Bring the Family
TO THE
HOMEMADE TABLE

WITH ITS CLASSIC RECIPES BUILT FOR ANYONE WHO LOVES food, coupled with a disarming girl-next-door tone, *Homemade with Love* will earn its place in the kitchens of everyone who craves an easier solution to preparing homemade meals for their family. Having long written on the pleasures of cooking from scratch, buying local, and eating at home on her blog In Jennie's Kitchen, Jennie Perillo shares her passion for farmers' markets and neighborhood shops while dishing out a hearty dose of practical culinary know-how for the working parent—or any time-strapped cook.

Gathering her family and friends together around the table has always been the most important part of her day, especially since the unexpected death of her husband, Mikey, in 2011. Though many things about her life were forever altered, her commitment to eating for nourishment—both physical and spiritual—has not.

Jennie has managed to reconcile sometimes time-consuming scratch cooking with her reality as a busy working parent of two. She's crafted shortcuts (like two homemade all-purpose baking mixes, used as a base for pancakes, muffins, and cupcakes) to make eating well just a little easier. Try recipes like Orange-Scented Waffles, Carrot Fennel Soup, Lentil Ricotta Meatballs, Strawberry Blender Sherbet, and Lemon Buttermilk Doughnuts. Memories of Mikey pervade the dinner table too, with Drop Biscuit Chicken Pot Pie, Apple, Cheddar & Pancetta Panini, and Linguine with White Clam Sauce. Simple, soulful recipes for every meal of the day emphasize farm fresh produce and whole foods. Jennie's distinctive voice extols the pleasures of eating close to home, and lingering around the table.

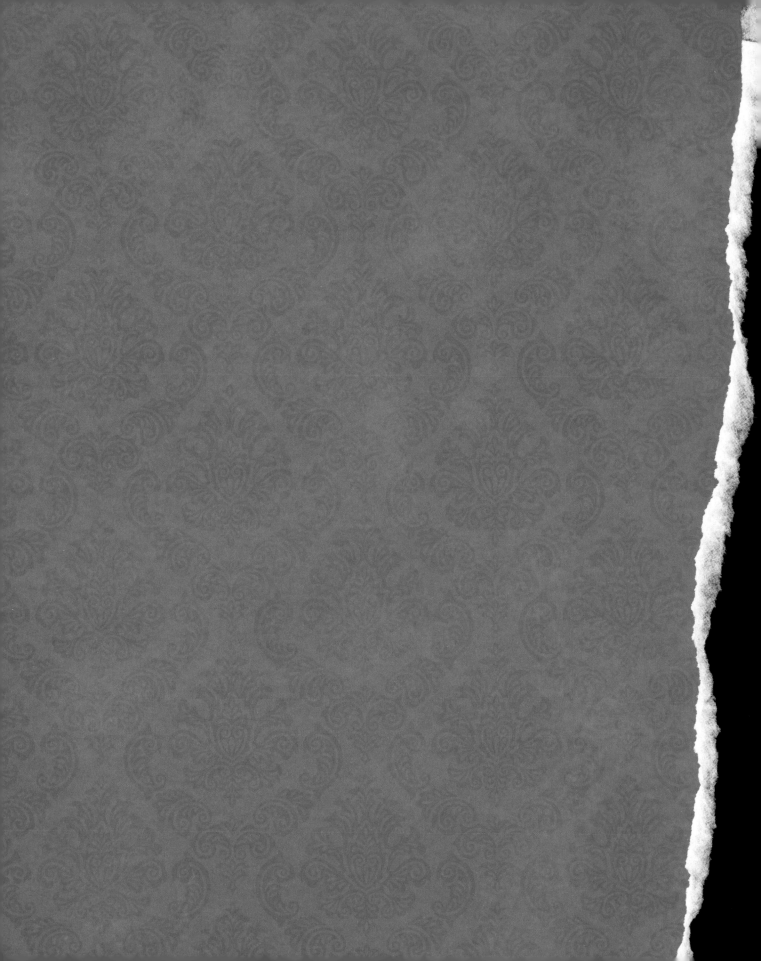

JENNIFER PERILLO
HOMEMADE
with
Love

SIMPLE SCRATCH COOKING *from* IN JENNIE'S KITCHEN

RUNNING PRESS
PHILADELPHIA · LONDON

Library of Congress Control Number: 2012942958

E-book ISBN 978-0-7624-4834-0

9   8   7   6   5   4   3   2   1
Digit on the right indicates the number of this printing

Cover and interior design by Amanda Richmond
Edited by Kristen Green Wiewora
Food Styling by Simon Andrews
Prop Styling by Mariellen Melker
Special thanks to Idan Bitton, Jay Kim, and *Saveur* magazine

Typography: Arno, Mailart Rubberstamp, and Jellyka Delicious Cake

Running Press Book Publishers
2300 Chestnut Street
Philadelphia, PA 19103-4371

Visit us on the web!
www.runningpresscooks.com

for
ISABELLA & VIRGINIA
dream big

Contents

Acknowledgments

Writing is not a solitary endeavor. While it is the author who finds the words to put to paper, it is life's experiences and the people around her who provide the inspiration. This is more than just a collection of recipes, it was a personal journey, and every word, every ingredient, brought me one step closer to a path towards healing. At times, it felt like it took an army of people to bring this lifelong dream from my kitchen to yours.

What started as encouragement from friends and family slowly grew from an idea into a reality. Thank you to Stacey Glick, my literary agent, for seeing I had what it takes—the heart, soul, and professional know-how to write this book. A good idea, solid recipes, and a well-crafted proposal are only half the work in writing a book—and at moments they feel like the toughest! After that, it takes foresight and faith from a publisher to help breathe life into it all. Kristen Green Wiewora, my editor at Running Press, recognized the potential in this project from the start. Thank you sounds so simple, and humble, and can never truly capture the deep gratitude I feel.

My first instinct is to call Amanda Richmond, the senior designer at Running Press, my designer, because she captured my essence—my style, look, and feel—so well, it's as though she knew me for years instead of mere months.

Penny De Los Santos—your gift and talent for making pictures is one I am so thankful to have had as a part of this book. Simon Andrews, Idan Bitton, Jay Kim, and Mariellen Melker—thank you for being part of those four magical days during the photo shoot, and thanks to *Saveur* for opening their test kitchen to us.

Thomas Conway, you're proof that not only can teachers make a difference, but they can also grow to become more than mentors—they can become friends for the rest of your life.

When I made the switch from the restaurant world into writing, Barbara Turvett took me under her wing at *Working Mother* magazine. Barbara, thank you for helping nurture my dreams, and recognizing I had what it takes to get this far.

Everyone should have a cheerleader as loud and encouraging as I do in my mom. I grew into a strong, resilient, headstrong woman thanks to her telling me every step of the way that no dream was too big or unachievable. Thank you, Mom, for loving and accepting me just as I am—that is the greatest gift any parent can bestow upon a child.

Cinderella may have only had one fairy godmother, but I was lucky enough to have two in my life. Auntie Joan and Aunt Barbara, thank you for being my guardian angels, both in life and in the kitchen.

Sometimes I have to pinch myself when I think about the amazing group of friends that surrounds me. Ilana Levine, Dominic Fumusa, Erin Patterson, Mike Canzoniero, Marina Babakoff, Vivian Manning-Schaffel, Brad Schaffel, Vania Kasper, John Kasper, Ilina Ewen, Gina Von Esmarch, Lindsay MacNaughton, David Leonard, Rosemary Flannery, Meryl Williams, Bryan Donovan, and Jeanise Vazquez—where would I be without all of your love, laughter, support, and appetites for everything I cook?

Diane Cu and Todd Porter, you both have been symbols of love, light, and faith in friendship in the face of anything life throws my way. You are my family, through and through.

C.G.—You're right: nothing is impossible.

Isabella and Virginia, home is always where the heart is, and mine is forever with the two of you. And to my shining star in the night sky... thank you for casting your brilliance and love in my life, Mikey.

1.

INTRODUCTION

Returning to Our Roots

When I was growing up, my mom cooked the red-check classics from scratch—meatballs, marinara sauce, chicken parmigiana—as any good Italian-American would've done. Any other cuisine, though, was fair game for shortcuts. The secret to her Asian pork chops was a packet of brown powdered gravy mix. Pancakes and frosted cakes always came out of a box. Mashed potatoes were more commonly found in the form of flakes—the task of peeling real ones was saved for Thanksgiving. Like many families in the '70s, we were told food should be convenient, and little by little real cooking became a special-occasion activity, vanishing from our weeknight routines.

Then roles reversed when I started high school. My parents divorced, and to keep us afloat my mom took a job as a supermarket cashier. We became a team, and I began helping out with dinner. I gravitated toward easy cooking techniques any 15-year-old who had never stepped into a kitchen could handle. Cooking this way also happened to be healthier, like grilling instead of frying and swapping in fresh vegetables for the canned counterparts that were a staple most of my youth. The seedlings of my desire to cook from scratch had been planted. I even started making homemade pizzas and stir-fries.

What began as baby steps in an attic apartment in Dyker Heights, Brooklyn, blossomed into my adult cooking style. I didn't need to let the boundaries of busy city living stop me from enjoying a slower-paced, from-scratch lifestyle in the kitchen. After college, I went on to work as a video producer, but food was always a grounding force. I'd come home after a day's work and settle in to cook a meal, just for myself. This love for nourishing myself morphed into a passion, and a way of expressing my affection for those close to me.

It took a life-changing moment, though, to realize feeding people was something I wanted to focus on full-time. My father died when I was twenty-four. He was diagnosed with pancreatic cancer the first week of January in 1998, and was gone less than three weeks later. The fleeting nature of life got me thinking about what I was doing with my own. Around that same time, my boyfriend Mikey, who would eventually become my husband, gave me a clipping from *Newsweek* magazine. It was about starting a personal chef business, and was exactly the inspiration I needed to connect the dots between my passion and my career. I slowly began to make a living as a personal chef, a food fairy god-mother of sorts, providing others with that magical twenty-fifth hour in the day that many people *think* they need to enjoy a home-cooked meal.

That part of my life seems so far away some days. Mikey, whom I talk about often on my blog, *In Jennie's Kitchen*, and throughout this cookbook, died suddenly in the summer of 2011 from an undiagnosed rare autoimmune disease called Goodpasture's syndrome. Before that fateful day on August 7, 2011, life was a busy balance of motherhood, marriage, and a career as a recipe developer and food writer.

My life changed in an instant, much the way you would turn a light switch on or off. Cooking played a big role in recovering some sense of normalcy in my life after his death. Aside from the most basic task of waking up to care for our young daughters, the thread that helped me keep it all together was cooking—it still is to this day. Cooking became my savior, and offered not only nourishment, but a sense of control in a world that seemed to no longer make sense.

Preparing a homemade meal has always been my release at the end of a long day. Sitting down at the table with our daughters, Isabella and Virginia, nourishes more than just our physical bodies. It creates a sense of connection and family, with each bite building a memory for the day when they branch out in their own directions.

HOW DID I GET HERE?

I didn't set out eight years ago to live such a pioneer lifestyle in the middle of New York City, making my own butter and mustard and buying locally milled flour. In fact, Mikey often teased me, saying, "When are you going to make your own water?" The problem was that I'd spoiled my palate working in the restaurants of world-class chefs like Tom Colicchio and Alain Ducasse. Those meals left a lasting impression on my taste buds, and the hauntingly good memories inspired me in my own kitchen.

Initially, parenthood challenged my love of cooking. Time became more precious, with every second competing for my attention. Yet, those memories of the way food was lovingly sourced and prepared influenced my own approach to feeding my family. The need to cook from scratch became a necessity, not a luxury. It seemed the most sensible and practical way to ensure I was serving the best-quality food that I could also afford.

I started simple with granola. It's a good example of how home cooking is both better for you and less expensive. The small batch brands, made with real ingredients and not loaded with corn syrup or sugar, are expensive for a reason. Businesses have to make back the cost of their ingredients, packaging, and labor before they can see any profit, hence the expensive price for a small package of granola made with high-quality ingredients. Buy the ingredients yourself, though, and you cut out the middle-man and keep the profit in your own pocket. Start by buying whatever you can in the bulk section of your supermarket to see the savings add up. When my local shop had organic old-fashioned oats on sale for seventy-nine cents per pound one month, the neighbors probably thought I was getting ready to launch a product line myself with the amount I started hoarding.

So, the first lesson for cooking from scratch—buying in bulk is your best friend. Even warehouse clubs carry some good-quality ingredients that make membership worthwhile, like King Arthur flour. If storage is an issue, find a friend to split the cost and the bounty.

Another reality of eating local on a budget is that it's a juggle every week. A few years back I realized buying local, ethically raised meat was taking up too much of my food budget. I decided it was better to eat it less often, and only from sources we believed to be living in a harmonious relationship with their land and animals. When we eat a piece of steak now, each morsel is cherished, not wolfed down. These are very personal decisions, and not "one size fits all." Make the choice that works best for *your* family and budget.

The one definitive thing I will say is this—if you want to cook, then you can. Yes, it's really that easy. Start off with the basics. Boil water for pasta, and brown some garlic in oil, then simmer it with tomatoes and fresh basil. It's satisfying, simple, and better than anything that will come from a jar or the frozen food section of the supermarket.

As you become more comfortable with ingredients and techniques, cooking will feel as second-nature as breathing. My first pizza crust twenty years ago came from a box: I just added water and oil to the mix. Now our Pizza Friday ritual at home begins with homemade dough made by mixing yeast, flour, salt, and water.

I'm constantly evolving as a home cook. Sometimes it's by design, but mostly it's from necessity. There's a term in the restaurant business called "cooking on the fly." It means to plan and cook a dish from whatever ingredients you have available. I've found it to be a good survival skill for handling many of life's curveballs, too.

2.

GETTING STARTED

Setting Up a Homemade Kitchen

Back when we first met, my husband had a strict rule: never leave IKEA without opening the packaging to make a quick count of the tools and pieces. That's a pretty good approach to cooking, too. Chefs call it their *mise en place*, a French phrase that means "putting in place." Does this mean I chop, measure, and set all my ingredients out before I start a recipe? In a perfect world that would be my approach, and when I'm in work mode, setting up a mise en place is essential to recording new recipes. When I'm donning my mom hat, though, my approach is more from the heart and less rigid. I prep as needed, and often the kids like lending a helping hand, too.

One rule I *always* follow before I set out to make any recipe is to check to make sure that I have all the ingredients. It may sound like a no-brainer, but how many times have you found yourself elbow-deep only to discover that someone nibbled on that bag of chocolate chips, or used the last drop of milk without telling you? So, really read through your recipe and make sure you have all your ingredients, including any special equipment you might need.

A few things to keep in mind while cooking your way through *Homemade with Love*:

- •**EGGS** are always large (50 grams), unless otherwise noted.

- •**BUTTER** is always unsalted, sometimes labeled "sweet cream" at the supermarket.

- •**SUGARS** can be granulated, natural cane, coarse, brown, and confectioners'. I use them all, so read the ingredient lists carefully.

- •**FLOURS** are like sugars: I don't use just one type. You'll find all-purpose, whole-wheat pastry, rye, and oat flour, plus my All-Purpose Baking Mixes (pages 20 and 22), so again, read the recipe through first.

•**MILK** is always whole, unless otherwise noted.

•**THERMOMETERS** are a baker and cook's best friend. Oven thermometers hang from the rack of your oven and are the best way to determine if it is heating to the proper temperature. Instant-read thermometers are used to measure the internal temperature of food, to make sure it is properly cooked.

THE PERFECT PANTRY

There's lots of talk about having a well-stocked pantry, but what does it mean, exactly? Simply put, my idea of a perfect pantry is one that allows me to serve my family homemade meals on a daily basis. Here's a little food for thought:

One day I found myself starving as I was in recipe-testing mode. I was surrounded by food—cakes and tarts, since it was berry season—but none of it made a meal. I kept putting off the inevitable act of eating because I thought I had no time. Finally, noon rolled around and I felt sure I was experiencing the moment at which I might actually go blind with hunger.

Then I remembered I had leftover roasted chicken in the fridge. I had also just canned some fresh pickles and made mayonnaise the day before. Suddenly, I found myself running around like an excited child when I realized the arugula in my backyard would be the perfect peppery partner. In less than five minutes, I had a gourmet-quality sandwich. Almost every ingredient was homemade or homegrown, except for the roll.

That's when I realized I didn't just wake up one day and know how to cook or love to eat. It's a relationship that has flourished over time. After years of finding my footing with ingredients, I'm now comfortable cooking on the fly. That's the beauty of cooking from scratch: combining the ingredients you have available with a few simple techniques to create a satisfying and comforting meal.

Now, I realize this little anecdote sounds idyllic. Take a deep breath, and find ease in knowing that I didn't always have a pantry filled with homemade condiments. Many of my garden experiments start with high hopes, but it's only through trial and error that I found arugula is a plant almost impossible to kill—seriously, my thumbs are far from green. I never gave up or gave in, though, and that's the message I want you to take away, too.

Don't set out to redo your pantry from top to bottom in a weekend. You'll get frustrated and feel like it's too time consuming. Take on projects as time allows, and little by little, you'll grow your pantry from store-bought staples like jarred mayonnaise into better-for-

you homemade options—see page 229 for a recipe to make your own low-fat mayo with egg whites! So, what do you say? Are you ready to build a better pantry?

For the Fridge

- **BUTTERMILK**—It sounds high in fat because it has butter in its name, but one cup only has two grams of fat, so don't be afraid to use it. I love the tang it adds to baked goods. I always prefer cultured buttermilk from the farmers' market because the flavor is better, and it doesn't have all the additives that the brands in the supermarket do. In a pinch, you can also make your own buttermilk substitute (just add 1 tablespoon of apple cider vinegar to a measuring cup, then fill it with milk to the one-cup mark).

- **BUTTER**— It's a staple in my pantry for making baked goods, but did you know butter can also be transformed into a savory condiment? "Compound butters" sound complicated, but are actually very easy to make, as you'll see with my Salted Molasses Butter on page 226.

- **CREAM**—Just a splash goes a long way, and it's an essential ingredient in homemade ricotta (page 32).

- **EGGS**—We eat a lot of eggs in my family, and for good reason—they're an inexpensive source of protein. For years, people feared high cholesterol and tossed the yolks. Now research shows the yolks are filled with choline, a nutrient key in brain development.

- **LEFTOVER WHITE OR BROWN RICE**—Yes, this one may sound silly, but once you make my Vegetable Fried Rice (page 96), you'll see why leftover rice is a must-have ingredient. Just make extra if you're cooking it for another meal, and you'll be enjoying the best Chinese takeout in the comfort of your own kitchen.

- **MILK**—A basic but necessary ingredient for many baking recipes. If you have a dairy or lactose allergy, or are vegan, I've found almond milk to be a great 1:1 substitute for cow's milk in baking.

- **ACTIVE DRY YEAST**—Restaurant-quality pizza is within reach as long as you keep this in stock (page 127).

- **DRIED SPICES**—Believe it or not, the cabinet above the stove is the worst place to store dried spices. If not used within a month or two, they'll become dull-tasting from the heat of the stove. Tucking them away in the fridge keeps them fresh and flavorful longer. My "must-haves"

HOMEMADE *with* Love

include dried parsley, dill, paprika, mustard powder, cinnamon, whole and ground nutmeg, coriander, chipotle powder, and cumin.

•**VEGETABLE BOUILLON**—Aside from the considerable savings—over $200 per year— making your own bouillon (a concentrated stock of sorts, page 24), is also a great way to use up extra vegetables and avoid preservatives. Being able to make a flavorful vegetable stock in minutes has saved me many a night when I'm running late with dinner.

•**PECORINO, PARMIGIANO REGGIANO, LOCATELLI, OR OTHER HARD ITALIAN GRATING CHEESE**—As an Italian-American, if given the choice between Parmesan and oxygen, I'd probably take my chances breathing. It adds a sharp note to everything from pasta with marinara sauce (page 27) to pizza (page 128) and lentil-ricotta meatballs (page 93). I'm talking about the real stuff, and it's okay to buy it already grated from the specialty cheese section of the supermarket. Just avoid any that's canned and "shelf-stable," which is closer to a science experiment than anything you should eat.

•**YOGURT**—Making my own (page 28) has been a big money saver. If you prefer to buy it, then opt for plain and add your own flavoring with honey or jams, as the fruit flavored ones tend to be filled with a lot of sugar. I often use Greek yogurt as an egg substitute in baked goods (¼ cup per egg), as in my Cherry Chocolate Chip Friendship Cookies (page 180).

Dry Goods

- **BAKING POWDER AND BAKING SODA**—If you love making muffins, cookies, biscuits, and cakes, then you'll need these leavening agents to make sure they rise properly. Baking powder should be replaced every year, but baking soda will stay active even with age.

- **BOXED PASTA**—I love making and eating homemade pasta (page 85), but I always keep a few boxes of good-quality store-bought pasta on hand when I need a quicker solution for mealtime.

- **DRIED BEANS AND LEGUMES**—There's nothing more satisfying than a pot of perfectly cooked beans. Lentils are often my go-to legume, since they're quick-cooking, and are the base to the best-ever vegetarian meatballs (page 93). But don't stop there: you can prepare a pot of your favorite beans and keep it in the fridge to use throughout the week (page 34). Look for them in the bulk foods section of your supermarket, as they are less expensive per pound than pre-packaged.

- **CANNED BEANS**— "Wait, didn't you just tell me to cook my beans from scratch?" This is where I admit as part of my twelve-step program that I'm human. I can't always conquer the world and get dinner ready by 5:30 p.m. without a few shortcuts. Yes, I love cooking beans from scratch, and will always argue that they taste better than their canned counterparts, but that doesn't mean you shouldn't still stock a few cans for back-up on nights when you're pressed for time. The kids love refried beans, so I always keep a can or two of pinto beans for those nights I'm in a rush and need to throw dinner together quickly. Canned chickpeas can get you out of a bind when you need a last-minute appetizer or healthy after school snack like hummus (page 158). They're also a great vegetarian source of protein.

- **CANNED TOMATOES**— Did I mention I am Italian? I'm pretty sure I would cease to exist without homemade marinara sauce at least once a week. I started preserving my own tomatoes three years ago, but I don't have the room to store a whole year's worth until the growing season starts up again, so canned tomatoes live side-by-side with my home-jarred ones. I prefer good-quality San Marzano tomatoes imported from Italy. Pastene's ground peeled tomatoes are my other favorite, and cost half the price. If you're concerned about consuming canned goods, Pomi has a tomato purée in BPA-free packaging.

HOMEMADE
with
Love

•**FLOURS**—Not a day goes by that I don't reach for a cup of flour, whether it's to make pancakes for breakfast (page 51), homemade pasta for dinner (page 85), or cookies for dessert (page 180). Be sure to buy an unbleached brand if using white flours. Many brands, including supermarket standards Gold Medal and Pillsbury's Best, are now unbromated (free of bromate, a potential carcinogen) as well. I keep an extensive collection of locally-milled whole grain flours too, including rye, spelt, and whole wheat pastry flour.

•**HONEY, AGAVE NECTAR, AND MAPLE SYRUP**—Use these to naturally sweeten hot tea, baked goods (page 172), salad dressings (page 231), and yogurt. Agave nectar is thinner and milder in taste than honey, making it a good substitute for simple syrup (page 203) in cold drinks like iced tea and lemonade (pages 203 and 202).

•**OLIVE OIL**—I buy extra-virgin. The taste of different brands varies like wine from different vineyards. Taste a few to find the one that best suits your palate.

•**TOMATO PASTE**—Canned tomato paste may seem inexpensive, but how many half-cans have gone to waste? Better to invest in the tube variety, which is double concentrated, so you can squeeze out as much or as little as you need. And don't forget, it's perishable, so store it in the refrigerator once it's opened.

•**VANILLA EXTRACT**—Skip the artificial imposters and invest in the real thing, which will be labeled "pure" vanilla extract. If you have a gluten allergy or sensitivity, read the label to make sure it's processed in a wheat-free facility. I load up on bottles of Nielsen-Massey, a certified gluten-free brand, when I visit the Williams-Sonoma outlet.

•**VINEGAR**—Balsamic and red wine vinegar are a must. Whisk them up with olive oil, salt, pepper, and a bit of honey and you'll never reach for a store-bought bottle of salad dressing again (page 231). Add apple cider vinegar to the list if you want to start canning and making savory jams like my tomato jam—it's incredibly addictive (page 216).

For the Freezer

• **BACON, SMOKED**—When I was a kid, bacon was reserved for breakfast. Now I know a little goes a long way, as you'll see in my Refried Lentils (page 148) and Smoky Corn and Bean Chili (page 98). I simply slice off what I need and keep the rest well-wrapped in the freezer. Pancetta, an Italian-style bacon, is a nice upgrade when your budget allows.

• **FROZEN VEGETABLES**—They're as nutritious as their fresh counterparts, and relying on them during the winter months is a good way to extend your local growing season. Frozen peas and corn mingle amongst the bags of fresh-frozen farmers' market berries and roasted vegetables in my freezer. There is a fine line between perfectly cooked frozen vegetables and a bowl of mush, so watch your cooking times carefully.

• **FROZEN ORGANIC FRUITS**—Smoothies are perhaps the quickest breakfast to make, and frozen fruit is the key. Most of the fruits that freeze well are also on the Environmental Working Group's (EWG) Dirty Dozen list for the highest use of pesticides, so I recommend buying these organic. If you buy fresh berries or peaches like I do from the farmers' market, be sure to talk to your farmers about their growing methods. They may be using pesticide-free and organic products even if they don't have the costly certification to call their produce organic.

• **GROUND BEEF**—Most meat at farmers' markets is frozen as soon as it's butchered. The best way to quickly thaw frozen meat is in a bowl of cold water set in the fridge. A one-pound package of ground beef is ready to use in about thirty minutes, and becomes the base for a quick meal of burgers and a salad, or one of my favorites—meatballs (page 102).

• **PANCAKES AND WAFFLES**—Nothing makes me happier than feeding the kids a homemade breakfast. It sets the tone for the rest of their day. I store leftover pancakes (page 51) and waffles (page 49) tightly wrapped in plastic in the freezer, and then pop them in the toaster for a quick reheat on busy mornings.

• **PIE & PASTRY DOUGH**—Trust me, when berries and peaches are in season, you'll be happy to have a batch of my Sweet Butter Crust on hand (page 174). It's also perfect for making hand pies to stow away in a picnic basket for summer outings (page 177).

HOMEMADE
with
Love

Guide to the Icons Used in this Book

PANTRY BASICS

FREEZER FRIENDLY

VEGETARIAN (No meat products, no fish)

VEGAN (No egg, no dairy, no meat products, no honey)

GLUTEN-FREE

MAKE AHEAD

UNDER ONE HOUR

30 MINUTES OR LESS

DAIRY-FREE

EGG-FREE

VEGETARIAN FRIENDLY

VEGAN FRIENDLY

GLUTEN-FREE ADAPTABLE

DAIRY-FREE ADAPTABLE

3.
Everyday BASICS

WHEN I WAS GROWING UP, AUNT JEMIMA'S MIX WAS the only way I knew to make pancakes or waffles. Now I keep all-purpose baking mixes ready to go in a canister to satisfy my daughters' hunger for fluffy, hot pancakes, which I'm pretty sure they'd eat for every meal if I let them. Personally, I have a soft spot for fresh-baked muffins, and thankfully the same mix makes it easy to bake up a batch of them within thirty minutes—a real bonus when berry season arrives.

When it comes to busy weeknights, all you need is twenty minutes to sit down and enjoy a stunningly simple bowl of tomato-basil sauce with pasta —and that includes time for boiling the water. Perhaps it's my Italian roots taking hold, but this is my go-to meal when I'm craving something hearty and satisfying, but am short on time. Come winter, there's nothing like a pot of homemade chicken soup, and starting with a homemade stock is key. While some people will tell you it has to simmer for hours, you'll start singing a different tune once you make my 60-Minute Chicken Stock (page 26) and learn my trick for coaxing maximum flavor in half the time.

ALL-PURPOSE BAKING MIX

I cooked my way through pancakes and waffles, then tackled cup-cakes, muffins, and more to give you the ultimate cooking-from-scratch shortcut—your own homemade, all-purpose baking mix. There's also no need for a dictionary to pronounce the ingredients list since there are no preservatives or artificial sweeteners, just good, wholesome ingredients you probably already have in the pantry.

MAKES 4 CUPS (619 GRAMS)

$3^3/_4$ cups (525 grams) unbleached all-purpose flour

$^1/_4$ cup (50 grams) granulated natural cane sugar

2 tablespoons (32 grams) baking powder

1 teaspoon (6 grams) baking soda

1 teaspoon (6 grams) fine sea salt

Add all the ingredients to a large bowl and whisk until well combined. Store in a tightly sealed container or plastic zip-top bags for up to 2 months. Ingredients will settle while stored, so be sure to stir it thoroughly, or shake well, before using.

STORAGE TIP: Label and date your All-Purpose Baking Mix. If you tend to go through a batch in a week, then make a double batch next time.

from left: Whole Grain Baking Mix (page 22), All-Purpose Baking Mix, and Homemade Oat Flour (page 22).

WHOLE GRAIN BAKING MIX

I love the earthy flavor whole grains add to baked goods. Just like my All-Purpose Baking Mix (page 20), this whole grain version makes getting breakfast together quicker and healthier. The banana and pecan studded pancakes (on page 51) are one of my favorites.

MAKES 4 CUPS (539 GRAMS)

2 cups (275 grams) whole wheat pastry flour

1 cup (109 grams) oat flour (recipe follows)

3/4 cup (87 grams) dark rye flour

4 teaspoons (24 grams) granulated natural cane sugar

2 tablespoons (32 grams) baking powder

1 teaspoon (6 grams) baking soda

1 teaspoon (6 grams) fine sea salt

Add all the ingredients to a deep bowl and whisk until well combined. Store in a tightly sealed container or plastic zip-top bags for up to 2 months. Ingredients will settle while stored, so be sure to stir it thoroughly, or shake well, before using.

HOMEMADE OAT FLOUR

Making oat flour at home is so easy, it almost sounds silly to call this a recipe, so let's call it a tip, okay? The technique is simple, requiring nothing more than a food processor. Old-fashioned rolled oats yield an equal amount of oat flour—one cup of oats yields one cup of oat flour. Feel free to make more or less, depending on how much oat flour you need.

MAKES 3 CUPS (270 GRAMS)

3 cups (270 grams) old-fashioned oats

Add the oats to the bowl of a food processor. Pulse 3 to 5 times to start breaking down the oats. Then turn the food processor on and let it run for 2 to 3 minutes, or until you have a fine, powdery flour. Store the flour in an airtight container or plastic zip-top bag for up to 1 month.

DIY GRANOLA

Granola was one of my husband's favorite foods. A handful served
dual purposes as both snack and breakfast, if he was patient enough to add it to a bowl with some milk. The ingredients used here can be bought in bulk, making it better on the budget. I love using pistachios and pumpkin seeds with dried cherries, but have left the recipe open, so you can taste test your way through the bulk bins to find your own favorite combination. I even make a few batches without dried fruit to use in my Granola & Berry Smoothies (page 45).

MAKES 6 TO 7 CUPS (660 GRAMS TO 770 GRAMS),
plus a few husband-size handfuls

3 cups (315 grams) old-fashioned rolled oats

1 cup (125 grams) raw unsalted nuts or seeds, such as shelled pistachios, sliced almonds, pecan halves, cashews, or pumpkin seeds

1 tablespoon (12 grams) flax seeds

1 tablespoon (11 grams) white or black sesame seeds

¼ teaspoon (1 gram) fine sea salt

½ teaspoon (2 grams) ground cinnamon

¼ cup (62 ml) extra-virgin olive oil

¼ cup (62 ml) pure maple syrup

2 cups (240 grams) dried fruit, such as raisins, dried cherries, currants, or diced apricots

Preheat the oven to 300°F (150°C).

In a large bowl, combine the oats, nuts, flax seeds, sesame seeds, salt, and cinnamon. Whisk together the olive oil and syrup, then pour over the dry ingredients. Stir until the mixture is well coated.

Spread the granola onto a rimmed 11-inch x 17-inch (28-cm x 43-cm) baking sheet. Bake for 30 minutes, stirring halfway through, until the oats and nuts are a deep golden color. Remove the granola from the oven, stir in the dried fruit, and set the tray on a wire rack to cool completely. Store in a tightly sealed jar for up to 2 weeks.

GLUTEN-FREE FRIENDLY This is easily adaptable to a gluten-free diet—just use a packaged variety of certified gluten-free oats, such as Bob's Red Mill. Bulk bins pose a risk for cross contamination, so be sure to buy certified gluten-free brands for your nuts, seeds, and dried fruits.

HOMEMADE VEGETABLE BOUILLON

I learned this technique for making bouillon from scratch from Heidi Swanson's blog, *101 Cookbooks*. I've saved tons of money and added a wealth of flavor to everything from soups, to stews, and pastas ever since. It may seem like a lot of salt, but remember, you're essentially curing the vegetables, and the salt ensures that they don't go rancid. I use a measured teaspoon of bouillon for each cup of water, but feel free to add more or less water to adjust the final flavor of the broth to your liking. Last note: I have a monster food processor (really, it's eleven cups), so you may need to make this in two batches if yours is smaller.

MAKES 1 QUART (645 GRAMS)

4 carrots, trimmed, scrubbed, and cut into large pieces

3 celery ribs, cut into 1/2-inch (1.25 cm) pieces

1 leek, white part only, sliced

1 small onion, cut into quarters

10 sun-dried tomato halves

1 1/2 cups (165 grams) cremini mushrooms (caps and stems), cleaned and cut into quarters

2 garlic cloves

Generous handful of fresh flat-leaf parsley, including stems, rinsed and patted dry

7 ounces (198 grams) kosher salt (I like Diamond Crystal)

1 teaspoon (4 grams) whole black peppercorns

Add all the ingredients to the bowl of a food processor. Pulse until it forms a wet paste and is well combined, about 5 minutes. Store in an airtight container in the refrigerator. The bouillon is ready to use after 1 week, which gives the flavors time to meld. It will keep for up to 3 months.

To use, combine 1 teaspoon bouillon with 1 cup of boiling water. If you prefer a clear consommé, place a fine-weave strainer over a bowl and pour the broth through the strainer. Discard the solids.

24

HOMEMADE

with

Love

HAVE IT YOUR WAY Need a low-sodium alternative? You can make this with less salt, or none if you wish, and simply store it in the freezer. Spoon it into ice cube trays and, once frozen, store the cubes in an airtight plastic zip-top bag for up to 2 months.

CLEANING LEEKS Leeks often have traces of dirt and grit, so be sure to clean them properly. Simply cut and discard the root end of the leek. Cut the leek in half lengthwise, and then rinse it under cold water until it is free of any dirt or grit.

PRESERVING 101 Mention "preserving food," and canning is what usually comes to mind, but there's more than one way to extend the life of your vegetables. In this instance, salt acts as the curing agent. As the bouillon sits in the fridge, the salt breaks the vegetables down (you'll notice it goes from coarse and grainy to quite wet and mushy over the course of the week while it's curing). Here, the salt is listed by weight because you need enough to make sure the vegetables cure properly, and so the salt can do its other important job—inhibit bacteria growth.

PANTRY BASICS · 30 MINUTES OR LESS · MAKE AHEAD · GLUTEN-FREE · FF · VEGAN

EVERY
DAY
BASICS

60-MINUTE CHICKEN STOCK

This has all the depth of flavor you'd expect from a long-simmered homemade stock, yet it's ready in just about an hour. The secret to this richly flavored chicken stock is browning the chicken in the pot before adding the water.

MAKES ABOUT 1½ QUARTS (1.5 L)

Kosher salt and freshly ground black pepper

3 pounds (1360 grams) bone-in and skin-on chicken thighs

1 tablespoon (15 ml) extra-virgin olive oil

1 medium onion, cut into quarters

4 carrots, sliced

2 celery stalks, sliced

3 garlic cloves

Handful of fresh flat-leaf parsley

1 dried bay leaf

HOMEMADE *with* Love

Season the chicken thighs with salt and pepper to taste. Heat the olive oil in a 4-quart stockpot over medium-high heat. Place the chicken skin-side down into the pot and cook in batches until nicely browned, about 5 to 7 minutes, without crowding the pan (you may need to do this in batches). Turn over and cook the other side until browned, 3 to 5 more minutes. Transfer the chicken to a deep bowl.

Add the onion, carrots, celery, and garlic to the pot and cook over medium-high heat until lightly golden and fragrant, 2 to 3 minutes. Return the chicken to the pot, along with the parsley and bay leaf. Add 6 cups of cold water and bring to a boil. Reduce heat to low—the stock should bubble gently—and cook for 40 minutes.

Using tongs or a large slotted spoon, remove the chicken from the pot and set aside. Pour the stock through a fine-weave strainer lined with cheesecloth. Discard the vegetables and herbs.

Let the chicken cool, then remove the meat from the bones and store it in a covered container in the refrigerator for up to 2 days (you can use it to make Twice As Nice Tacos, page 109, or Red Grape and Dill Chicken Salad, page 67). Divide the stock into small containers and let it cool completely before covering and storing in the refrigerator for up to 3 days, or in the freezer for up to 2 months.

20-MINUTE MARINARA SAUCE

Serve this simply over pasta, or keep it on hand for pizza night—
this marinara sauce has been my dinner "lifejacket" on many a busy weeknight. It easily doubles and triples, so make extra to keep your freezer well stocked.

MAKES ABOUT 1 QUART (900 GRAMS)

1 tablespoon (15 ml) extra-virgin olive oil
2 garlic cloves
1 (28-ounce/784 grams) can whole peeled San Marzano tomatoes
Handful of fresh basil leaves, torn into pieces
Sea salt and freshly ground black pepper

Heat the olive oil in a 2-quart (2-L) pot over medium heat. Add the whole garlic cloves and cook until fragrant and golden, 1 to 2 minutes, shaking the pot once or twice so the garlic browns evenly.

Using your hands, squeeze the tomatoes over the pot. (Alternatively, you can break the tomatoes up into a bowl if you're worried about oil popping up when the liquid makes contact with the hot oil, or you can purée the tomatoes in a blender for a smoother sauce.) Add the remaining liquid from the can. Add the basil, season with the salt and pepper to taste, and stir. Reduce the heat to medium-low and let cook for 15 minutes. If not using immediately, let the sauce cool completely before storing it in the refrigerator (it will stay fresh for up to 3 days).

SEASONAL SWAP-IN Substitute a teaspoon of basil pesto (page 87) during the winter months when fresh basil is not in season.

FREEZE IT! Store cooked marinara sauce in an airtight container in the freezer for up 2 months.

HOMEMADE YOGURT

Wouldn't it be great if you could multi-task during your sleeping hours, too? Well, you can, at least when it comes to making yogurt. All the work is done overnight simply by leaving the light on in your oven. One taste and you'll find it hard to go back to the store-bought stuff. This recipe makes a thin yogurt, which you can drain in a double layer of cheesecloth if you prefer it thicker (see sidebar, below). Once you make your first batch, be sure to set aside three tablespoons of the yogurt to use as the starter for your next batch.

MAKES ABOUT 1 PINT (448 GRAMS)

2 cups (500 ml) whole or reduced-fat milk
3 tablespoons (48 grams) plain yogurt with live active cultures

Turn the light on inside your oven to "preheat" it 30 minutes before starting.

Pour the milk into a 2-quart (2-L) pot and heat it over a low flame until it registers 170ºF (76ºC). It should be steaming but not boiling. Remove the pot from the stove and let it sit until it cools to between 105ºF (40ºC) and 110ºF (43ºC).

Meanwhile, set the starter yogurt out to let it come to room temperature.

Stir the yogurt into the cooled milk, whisking thoroughly, and pour into a clean, sterilized quart-sized glass jar. Screw the top onto the jar. Place the jar on a rimmed baking sheet in the center rack of the oven for 8 hours until it is set, resembling a loose gelatin. Give it a stir, and don't worry that it seems too liquid. It will thicken slightly as it cools in the fridge. Cover tightly and chill for at least 6 hours, or overnight, before using. The yogurt will keep for up to 1 week in the fridge.

> **GO GREEK** If you prefer a thicker yogurt, place a piece of fine-woven cheesecloth in a strainer set over a bowl, and pour the yogurt into the strainer. Let it sit overnight in the refrigerator and get ready to wake up to homemade Greek-style yogurt.

PANTRY BASICS · MAKE AHEAD · V · EGG-FREE · GLUTEN-FREE

HOMEMADE CASHEW MILK

Some twenty years ago, I toured the Natural Gourmet Cookery School in New York City. The school's name has since changed to the Natural Gourmet Institute, but the memory of my first sip of homemade almond milk is still the same—creamy, sweet, and nothing like the commercially packaged versions. I've been making my own almond milk for a few years now, but it was while testing recipes for this book that I decided it was time to swap cashews into my normal almond milk recipe, too.

There are no special tools required—all you need is a blender and fine-weave cheesecloth, which can be found in most supermarkets next to the disposable aluminum pans or where the foil and plastic wrap are stocked. If you get hooked on making this often, like I did, you can buy special nut milk bags online or at health food stores that allow you to strain the milk only once to remove the pulp.

MAKES 3 CUPS (750 ML)

$^1\!/_2$ cup (200 grams) raw unsalted cashews
3 cups (750 ml) filtered or purified water

Add the cashews and water to the bowl of a blender. Blend on high speed until mostly smooth, about 5 minutes. Set a strainer over a deep bowl, and line it with a fine-weaved cheesecloth (alternatively, you can use a nut milk bag found in health food stores, and you'll only need to strain it once). Pour the milk through, using a rubber spatula to press as much milk from the solids as possible. Pour the strained milk through the cheesecloth two more times to remove all the pulp. Discard the solids, and store the milk in a covered container, in the refrigerator, for up to 1 week. Shake well before each use.

WHY FILTERED OR PURIFIED WATER? Living in New York City, I have access to very safe drinking water straight from the tap. If you have any doubts about the quality of your local drinking water, then it's best to use filtered or purified water.

HOW TO USE CASHEW MILK Pour it over your cereal, steam it for your morning latte, swap it in for whatever amount of milk is called for in a recipe—these are just a few ideas for cashew milk. Basically, you can use this as you would any other milk, but keep in mind it has a slightly sweeter flavor.

HOMEMADE NUT BUTTERS

Making peanut butter at home may seem like a natural thing to do,
but what about other types of nuts? Cashew butter makes for an equally delicious pairing with jam, and I particularly like the sweet undertones of walnut butter slathered on a slice of toast.

Cashew Butter

MAKES 1 CUP (254 GRAMS)

2 cups (270 grams) roasted, unsalted cashews

Grapeseed or canola oil, as needed

$1/4$ teaspoon (1 gram) fine sea salt

Add the cashews to the bowl of a food processor. Pulse for 1 minute to break down the nuts slightly. Add a few drops of oil and salt, then process until smooth, 6 to 7 minutes, scraping down the sides of the food processor as necessary. Store in an airtight jar, at room temperature, for up to 2 weeks.

Walnut Butter

MAKES 1 CUP (190 GRAMS)

2 cups (200 grams) unsalted walnuts

$1/4$ teaspoon (1 gram) fine sea salt

Preheat the oven to 350ºF (180ºC).

Place the walnuts on a rimmed baking sheet and bake until fragrant and lightly golden, 5 to 7 minutes. Remove the baking sheet from the oven, and set aside until walnuts are completely cooled.

Place the cooled walnuts in the bowl of a food processor. Pulse for 1 minute to break them down slightly. Season with the salt, then process until smooth, 3 to 4 minutes, scraping down the sides of the food processor as necessary. Store in an airtight jar, at room temperature, for up to 1 week.

CREAMY HOMEMADE RICOTTA

I had my first taste of fresh ricotta about ten years ago, and the crazy thing is I don't remember exactly where it was from. The experience was enough, though, to make me swear off the commercial stuff that I'd known all my life until that point. Luckily, I live in an Italian neighborhood with a couple of family-owned markets that make fresh ricotta. The only problem is that fresh ricotta can be an expensive habit to have, so as I delved deeper into cooking everything from scratch, I wondered if I could make it myself. There are a lot of recipes online now for homemade ricotta, but what makes this one really special is its creamy texture, which comes from using whole milk and heavy cream. My other trick is using buttermilk, which I think makes for a softer curd than using fresh lemon juice.

MAKES ABOUT 2 CUPS (400 GRAMS)

4 cups (1 L) whole milk
1 cup (250 ml) heavy cream
$^3/_4$ cup (187 ml) buttermilk
$^1/_2$ teaspoon (3 grams) fine sea salt

HOMEMADE *with* *Love*

Combine the milk, cream, buttermilk, and salt in a 4-quart pot over medium heat. Bring to a gentle, not rolling, boil. As the curds begin to separate from the whey, you'll see little white flecks pop to the surface and the milk will turn into a cloudy, watery-looking liquid. Let it cook for 1 to 2 more minutes until larger curds begin to form, then remove the pot from the heat. Place it on a back burner and let it sit for 30 minutes to help the curds develop further.

Meanwhile, line a sieve or fine mesh strainer with a few layers of cheesecloth and place it over a deep bowl or pot. Spoon the curds into the cheesecloth-lined strainer. Resist the temptation to pour it into the strainer all at once. Gently ladling the curds keeps them fluffy. Once all the curds have been ladled into the strainer, pull the sides of the cheesecloth up and over the ricotta to cover it so it doesn't dry out or form a skin on top. Let it sit in the cheesecloth to drain the excess liquid for 15 to 30 minutes. The length of time you drain it depends on how creamy you'd like your ricotta—the longer, the drier. If using it in a baked recipe, you'll want a drier texture. If serving it "straight up" on a cheese board or spreading it on toast, you'll want it to be on the creamier side. The ricotta may be stored in a covered container in the refrigerator for up to 2 days.

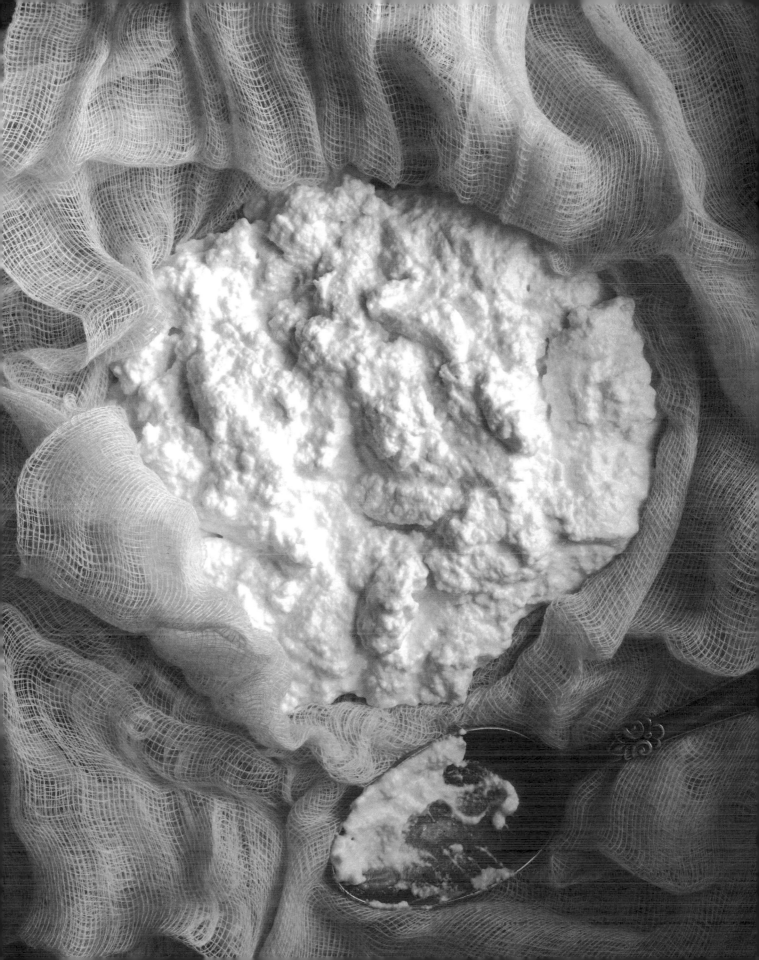

A POT OF BEANS

There's nothing fussy or difficult about cooking beans from scratch.
It's what you add to the pot that elevates them from a humble ingredient to culinary excellence. Using olive oil in the water adds a creaminess to the cooked beans. The cooking liquid becomes quite flavorful too, so you should think of this as a "bean stock"—I often swap it in for chicken and vegetable stock in soups and sauces.

Freshness counts when it comes to the cooking time. Most recipes call for soaking or long cooking times because bags of beans on supermarket shelves tend to be older. They need more time to rehydrate. Seeking out fresher dried beans at your local farmers' market not only results in a better flavor—it also reduces the cooking time significantly.

MAKES ABOUT 3 CUPS (630 GRAMS)

1 cup dried beans (185 grams), picked over, rinsed, and soaked overnight, if needed (dried beans from the farmer's market may not need the soak, depending on freshness)

¼ cup (62 ml) extra-virgin olive oil

2 garlic cloves, smashed

Handful of fresh flat-leaf parsley, rinsed

¼ teaspoon (1 gram) sea salt

⅛ teaspoon freshly ground black pepper

Combine all the ingredients in a 4-quart (4-L) pot and add 4 cups (1 L) of cold water. Bring to a boil over medium-high heat, then reduce the flame to the lowest setting. Cover the pot and let the beans cook at a gentle simmer until tender, about 1 hour.

Remove the pot from the heat and let the beans cool in the pot. Transfer to a container with the cooking liquid, cover, and store in the refrigerator for up to 1 week, or freeze for up to 2 months.

MAKE AHEAD · PANTRY BASICS · VEGAN · GLUTEN-FREE

PARMESAN SKILLET CROUTONS

For years I made croutons by baking them in the oven. Then one day
I was at my friend Vania's house and began nibbling on a bowl of croutons set out on the kitchen counter. The seasoning clung to the chunks of bread so perfectly, and they were the crunchiest croutons I'd ever tasted. I asked her secret, and she told me it was actually her mom's—Chari cooks them in a skillet on the stovetop. I haven't baked a crouton since that day!

MAKES 2 CUPS (80 GRAMS)

2 cups (80 grams) cubed day-old baguette

1 teaspoon (2 grams) finely chopped fresh flat-leaf parsley

2 tablespoons (6 grams) grated Parmesan cheese

Sea salt and freshly ground black pepper, to taste

1 tablespoon (15 ml) extra virgin olive oil

Toss all of the ingredients together in a bowl until the bread cubes are well coated.

Heat an 8-inch (20 cm) skillet over medium heat. Add the seasoned bread cubes to the pan and cook, turning occasionally, until golden all over, 5 to 7 minutes. Store in an airtight container for up to 3 days.

GOT CROUTONS? These are quite addictive, and I used to have to shoo Mikey away once they were done to be sure I had enough for whatever recipe I'd planned to use them in. The good news is the recipe is easy to double: just be sure to use a larger pan—10 to 12-inch (25 cm to 30 cm)—and keep in mind the cooking time may be slightly longer.

EGG-FREE · 30 MINUTES OR LESS · V · MAKE AHEAD

4.

Breakfast
ON THE GO

IT MAY BE A CLICHÉ, BUT BREAKFAST REALLY IS THE most important meal of the day. It's the difference between starting the day with a full tank of gas and the needle on empty. Personally, I'm an egg girl, and need the protein boost to get going.

Sometimes you have to scoot out in a rush, but it doesn't mean you can't treat yourself to something homemade. I'll make a quick batch of muffins before bed when I know the next morning will be a busy one. Some pastries, like scones (page 40), freeze well and just need a quick reheat in the toaster. Smoothies (page 45) are another perfect on-the-go meal, and perk me up more than a cup of coffee.

ORANGE-SCENTED
CHOCOLATE CHUNK SCONES

A good scone is hard to find, even in a food capital like New York City.
Many tend to be too cakey or too dry, and almost all of them are oversized. Not these scones, folks. These have a moist, crumbly texture, can be eaten in four or five bites, and come with a bonus—they're dotted with bittersweet chocolate and a whisper of orange.

MAKES ONE DOZEN

$1/2$ cup (125 ml) plus 1 tablespoon (15 ml) buttermilk

1 large egg

1 cup (138 grams) whole wheat pastry flour

1 cup (145 grams) unbleached all-purpose flour, plus more for dusting

$1/4$ cup (50 grams) granulated natural cane sugar

1 tablespoon (15 grams) baking powder

$1/4$ teaspoon (1 gram) fine sea salt

Freshly grated zest of 1 orange

6 tablespoons (84 grams) very cold unsalted butter, cut into 12 pieces

4 ounces (112 grams) bittersweet chocolate, coarsely chopped

1 teaspoon (6 grams) coarse natural cane sugar (optional)

Preheat the oven to 425°F (220°C).

Using a fork, lightly beat $1/2$ cup of the buttermilk with the egg in a small bowl. Set aside.

Add the flours, granulated sugar, baking powder, salt, and orange zest to a deep medium-sized bowl. Whisk to combine. Scatter the butter on top of the dry ingredients and rub together quickly with your fingers until it forms a sandy-looking texture with some pebble-sized pieces.

Add the chocolate, and stir well to combine.

Pour in the buttermilk-egg mixture. Using a fork, stir together until it forms a crumbly-looking dough.

Turn the dough out onto a lightly floured counter. Knead it once or twice until the dough is smooth. Divide the dough in half, and shape each piece into two circles, $1/2$ inch (1.5 cm) thick. Use a sharp knife to cut each circle into 6 wedges (as if cutting a pizza).

Place the scones on an ungreased baking sheet. Brush with the remaining tablespoon of buttermilk and sprinkle the tops with the coarse sugar, if desired.

Bake for 12 minutes until the bottoms are lightly browned and the tops are golden. Remove from the oven and set the tray on a wire rack to cool a few minutes before serving. Leftovers may be stored in an airtight container at room temperature up to 2 days. Heat them up in the toaster to crisp the scones before serving. To freeze leftovers, wrap them tightly in plastic wrap and foil. Let frozen scones thaw in the fridge overnight, and reheat in the toaster before serving.

FF UNDER 1 HOUR V

DRIED CHERRY & PISTACHIO SCONES

I love dried cherries, so I try to work them into recipes as much as possible. While creating this one, I spied the pistachios sitting on the shelf and couldn't help but add a "Mikey" touch. Pistachios were his favorite nut, and they've become a recurring theme in my recipes. The base of these scones serves as a blank canvas for any dried fruit and nuts you like, though, so feel free to put your own spin on it. Try swapping in dried cranberries or currants for the cherries, and almonds for the pistachios, or leaving the nuts out altogether.

MAKES ONE DOZEN

$^1/_2$ cup (125 ml) plus 1 tablespoon (15 ml) buttermilk

1 large egg

1 cup (138 grams) whole wheat pastry flour

1 cup (145 grams) unbleached all-purpose flour, plus more for dusting

$^1/_4$ cup (50 grams) granulated natural cane sugar

1 tablespoon (15 grams) baking powder

$^1/_4$ teaspoon (1 gram) fine sea salt

Freshly grated zest of 1 lemon

6 tablespoons (84 grams) very cold unsalted butter, cut into 12 pieces

$^1/_2$ cup (74 grams) shelled pistachios, toasted and chopped

$^1/_2$ cup (87 grams) dried sour cherries, coarsely chopped

1 teaspoon (6 grams) coarse natural cane sugar (optional)

Preheat the oven to 425ºF (220ºC).

Using a fork, lightly beat $^1/_2$ cup of the buttermilk and the egg together in a small bowl. Set aside.

Add the flours, granulated sugar, baking powder, salt, and lemon zest to a deep medium-sized bowl. Whisk to combine. Scatter the butter on top of the dry ingredients and rub together quickly with your fingers, until it forms a sandy-looking texture with some pebble-sized pieces. Add the pistachios and cherries, stirring to mix thoroughly. Pour in the buttermilk-egg mixture, and stir together with a fork until it forms a crumbly-looking dough.

Turn the dough out onto a lightly floured counter. Knead it once or twice to give the dough a smoother appearance. Divide the dough in half, and shape it into two circles, $^1/_2$ inch (1.5 cm) thick. Use a sharp knife to cut each circle into 6 wedges (as if cutting a pizza).

Place the scones on an ungreased baking sheet. Brush with the remaining tablespoon of buttermilk and sprinkle the tops with the coarse sugar, if desired. Bake for 12 minutes until the bottoms are lightly browned and the tops are golden. Remove from the oven and set the tray on a wire rack to cool for a few minutes before serving. Leftovers may be stored in an airtight container at room temperature up to 2 days. Heat them up in the toaster to crisp the scones before serving. To freeze leftovers, wrap them tightly in plastic wrap and foil. Let frozen scones thaw in the fridge overnight, and reheat in the toaster before serving.

UNDER 1 HOUR   V

ZUCCHINI WALNUT MUFFINS

Just around the time spring morphs into summer, zucchini makes its appearance at the farmers' markets. It is one of my favorite moments, next to berry season. I love simply slicing them into coins, sautéing them in a little olive oil, and serving them with a bit of grated Parmesan cheese. There's also the Zucchini Ribbon Salad with Grape Tomatoes & Basil on page 70, which is a favorite that requires no cooking at all. But those are savory dishes, and since I love squash as much as I do, I had to find a way to work it into breakfast, too.

MAKES 18 MUFFINS

2^1/$_2$ cups (360 grams) whole wheat pastry flour

1 teaspoon (5 grams) baking powder

^{1}/$_2$ teaspoon (3 grams) baking soda

^{1}/$_2$ teaspoon (3 grams) fine sea salt

^{1}/$_2$ teaspoon (1 gram) ground allspice

^{1}/$_2$ teaspoon (2 grams) ground cinnamon

^{3}/$_4$ cup (150 grams) packed light or dark brown sugar

Freshly grated zest of 1 lemon

1^1/$_2$ cups (153 grams) shelled walnuts, coarsely chopped

3 large eggs

^{1}/$_2$ cup (125 ml) canola oil

2^1/$_4$ cups (283 grams) shredded zucchini (about 2 medium squash)

2 teaspoons (12 grams) coarse granulated natural cane sugar

Preheat the oven to 375°F (190°C). Line 12-cup and 6-cup muffin tins with paper liners.

Whisk the flour, baking powder, baking soda, salt, allspice, cinnamon, and brown sugar together in a large bowl. Add the lemon zest and walnuts, and stir to combine.

In a separate small bowl, lightly beat the eggs and the canola oil. Pour over the flour mixture and stir with a wooden spoon until well mixed with the dry ingredients (it will look more like a loose dough than a batter). Fold in the zucchini.

Evenly spoon the batter into the prepared muffin tins and sprinkle the tops with the coarse sugar. Bake one tray at a time until the tops are golden and a skewer inserted comes out clean, 18 to 22 minutes. Let the muffins rest in the tin for 5 minutes, then remove from the tray and transfer to a wire rack to cool (this helps avoid soggy muffin bottoms).

CLEMENTINE & PISTACHIO CRUMB MUFFINS

In my opinion, a muffin should be light and airy, have a little bit of texture, and be no larger than the size of a fist—my fist, that is, not the Hulk's. This muffin delivers on all those fronts. The sweet scent of fresh clementine and an ever-so-tender crumb give it a dainty quality. The crumb topping studded with bits of pistachio makes for a playful, rugged contrast. It's everything a muffin should be, as far as I'm concerned.

MAKES ONE DOZEN

FOR THE TOPPING:

- ½ cup (75 grams) unbleached all-purpose flour
- 2 tablespoons (32 grams) packed dark brown sugar
- ⅛ teaspoon fine sea salt
- ⅛ teaspoon ground cloves
- ¼ cup (37 grams) shelled, raw pistachios, finely chopped
- 3 tablespoons (42 grams) unsalted butter, melted

FOR THE MUFFINS:

- 2 cups (290 grams) All-Purpose Baking Mix (page 20)
- ¼ cup (50 grams) granulated natural cane sugar
- Grated zest of 2 clementines
- 6 tablespoons (84 grams) cold unsalted butter, cut into 12 pieces
- 1 cup (250 ml) milk
- Freshly squeezed juice of 2 clementines, about ⅓ cup (83 ml)

Preheat the oven to 350°F (180°C). Line a 12-cup muffin tin with paper liners.

To make the crumb topping, add the flour, brown sugar, salt, and cloves to a small bowl, and whisk to combine. Add the pistachios. Pour the butter over the mixture and stir with a fork to mix well until it looks like a wet, pebbly sand.

To make the muffin batter, add the baking mix, granulated sugar, and zest to a medium bowl. Whisk to combine. Scatter the butter pieces on top, and vigorously rub with your fingertips until it forms a sandy, pebbly mixture. Pour the milk and juice over the flour mixture. Using a wooden spoon, stir until the batter is just mixed and there are no visible traces of flour. Evenly spoon the batter into the cups of the prepared muffin tin. Sprinkle the tops with an even amount of the crumb topping.

Bake until golden brown and a skewer inserted in the center comes out clean, 25 to 27 minutes. Remove from the oven and set on a wire rack to cool slightly before serving.

IN A PINCH If you want to make these muffins past clementine season, you can swap in Mandarin zest and juice. Orange zest and juice work well, too, if you really have a craving for these muffins but can't find clementines or Mandarin oranges.

42

HOMEMADE with Love

 EGG-FREE UNDER 1 HOUR V

LEMON BLUEBERRY MUFFINS

Nothing beats a handful of fresh-picked blueberries for snacking, but when it comes to muffins, I find frozen is the way to go. You can either freeze your own when they're in season—just store them in plastic zip-top bags—or buy a bag in the frozen food aisle. Wild blueberries are my favorite for these muffins, and luckily my local Costco sells five-pound bags of Wyman's Maine Wild Blueberries, so I always have them on hand.

MAKES ONE DOZEN

2 cups (290 grams) All-Purpose Baking Mix (page 20)
3/4 cup (150 grams) granulated natural cane sugar
Grated zest of 2 lemons
1 stick (112 grams) unsalted butter, cut into 16 pieces
1 cup (250 ml) milk
1 large egg
1 1/2 cups (165 grams) frozen blueberries
2 teaspoons (12 grams) coarse natural cane sugar

HOMEMADE *with Love*

Preheat the oven to 350ºF (180ºC). Line a 12-cup muffin tin with paper liners.

In a large bowl, whisk together the baking mix, granulated sugar, and lemon zest to combine. Scatter the butter pieces over the mixture and quickly rub between your fingers until it forms a sandy-looking mixture (alternatively, you can use a pastry blender for this step).

In a separate small bowl, beat the milk and egg together with a fork until well mixed. Pour over the flour mixture and, using the same fork, stir until the batter is just combined, and there are no visible traces of flour. Using a rubber spatula, fold in the blueberries.

Fill each muffin cup with a generous 1/3 cup of the batter. Evenly sprinkle the tops with the coarse sugar. Bake until golden, and a skewer inserted in the center comes out mostly clean, 27 to 29 minutes. The sugar will form a nice "crust" on top of the muffins.

GRANOLA & BERRY SMOOTHIE

I love starting the day with a smoothie, but sometimes feel like I need a little more substantial "stick to your ribs" breakfast. That's where a bit of granola (page 23) comes in handy. Toasted old-fashioned oats are also an easy substitution if you're all out of granola but still want to add an extra boost to your breakfast.

SERVES ONE

¹/₂ cup (55 grams) Homemade Granola,
  preferably without dried fruit (page 23)

1 cup (115 grams) frozen strawberries

1 cup (225 ml) milk

Add all the ingredients to a blender. Blend until smooth, 1 to 2 minutes. Serve immediately.

CUSTOMIZE IT! Allergic to dairy? No problem: just swap in soy milk, coconut milk, or almond milk. All out of strawberries? Try using frozen blueberries, blackberries, or raspberries.

GLUTEN-FREE · 30 MINUTES OR LESS · V · VEGAN FRIENDLY · EGG-FREE

5.

Hot BREAKFASTS

A STEAMING CUP OF COFFEE AND A HOT BREAKFAST make starting the day more bearable—especially Mondays. Pancakes are a no-brainer with a scoop of my All-Purpose Baking Mix (page 20), and frittatas are great make-ahead meals that reheat incredibly well. I've even been known to pop a slice in the toaster when I'm feeling particularly slow-moving in the morning and want an easy cleanup.

When time allows, there's nothing more soothing than starting the day with a perfectly poached egg (page 58). Back when Virginia, my youngest daughter, was two years old, our favorite mornings were the lazy ones when we poked at the eggs with toasted points—toasted bread cut into triangles—and watched the bright orange yolks dribble out onto the plate.

VANILLA BLUEBERRY WAFFLES

When I created this recipe, my friend Bryan was helping me in the test kitchen. We had just finished making the Orange-Scented Waffles (page 50), and I turned to him and asked if we should try a blueberry version. He looked at me and said, "You mean like the ones they sell in the frozen foods aisle"? This is a hundred times better than anything that comes out of a box, but if you must know, yes, that is exactly what I had in mind.

MAKES 10 (4-INCH/10-CM SQUARE) WAFFLES

1 cup (250 ml) buttermilk
2 large eggs, beaten
4 tablespoons (56 grams) unsalted butter, melted
1 teaspoon (5 ml) vanilla extract
1¹/₂ cups (215 grams) All-Purpose Baking Mix (page 20)
I cup (125 grams) frozen blueberries

In a medium bowl, beat the buttermilk, eggs, butter, and vanilla with a fork until well mixed. Add the baking mix, and stir until just combined and there are no visible traces of flour. Gently fold in the blueberries. Let the batter sit for 5 minutes.

Grease the waffle iron if it is not nonstick. Scoop batter onto each waffle mold, filling it by two thirds. The amount of batter you will need depends on the size and type of your waffle iron. Close the waffle maker and cook the waffles according to the manufacturer's directions. Serve the waffles immediately, or see the recipe sidebar for tips on storing and reheating them.

EASY EATS Hot breakfasts are ready with the push of a button—the one on your toaster! Make a double batch of waffles, and let leftover waffles cool completely. Then place them in a plastic zip-top bag, removing as much air as possible, and store them in the freezer. On busy mornings, pop them in the toaster and get ready for the quickest homemade hot breakfast ever.

MAKE AHEAD · V · 30 MINUTES OR LESS

ORANGE-SCENTED WAFFLES

Any time a boring baked good needs a little boost or a makeover, I reach for whatever citrus I have on hand. All it takes is some freshly grated zest to liven up muffins, pancakes, or in this case, waffles. The kids perked up the first time I served these waffles, asking what I did differently—that's how I knew I had a winner on my hands.

MAKES ONE DOZEN (4-INCH/10-CM SQUARE) WAFFLES

2^{1}/$_{4}$ cups (285 grams) Whole Grain Baking Mix (page 22)

Freshly grated zest of 2 oranges

1^{1}/$_{4}$ cups (312 ml) milk

2 large eggs, beaten

4 tablespoons (56 grams) unsalted butter, melted

Preheat the waffle iron.

Whisk the baking mix and orange zest together in a deep bowl. Combine the buttermilk, eggs, and butter in a separate bowl. Beat with a fork until well mixed. Pour into the bowl with the dry ingredients, and stir until just combined and there are no visible traces of flour. Let the batter sit for 5 minutes.

Grease the waffle iron if it is not nonstick. Scoop batter onto each waffle mold, filling it by two thirds. The amount of batter you will need depends on the size and type of your waffle iron. Close the waffle maker, and cook the waffles according to the manufacturer's directions. Serve the waffles immediately, or see page 49 for tips on storing and reheating them.

> **WASTE NOT, WANT NOT** Once citrus is zested, the rest of the fruit will dry out pretty quickly, so be sure to juice it so nothing goes to waste. If you plan on using it within a few days, you can keep it in the fridge in a tightly sealed container. Otherwise, I keep a few ice cube trays in the freezer to store the juice in. Once the cubes are frozen, transfer them to a labeled plastic zip-top bag. Thaw the cubes as needed for recipes (page 208), or use them to add a hint of flavor to water, seltzer, or cocktails.

MAKE
AHEAD

V

30
MINUTES
OR LESS

FLUFFY BUTTERMILK PANCAKES

Breakfast was sometimes a battle on Sunday mornings because my husband loved waffles, but our daughter Isabella always wanted pancakes. I don't blame her, as these are particularly light and, well, fluffy, as they're aptly named. Cooking them in a bit of butter is the key to achieving that crisp ring around the edge.

MAKES 8 TO 10 PANCAKES

1 cup (145 grams) All-Purpose Baking Mix (page 20)

$^3/_4$ cup (187 ml) buttermilk

1 large egg

2 tablespoons (28 grams) unsalted butter, melted, plus more for greasing the pan

$^1/_2$ teaspoon vanilla extract

Add the baking mix to a medium bowl. Pour the buttermilk, egg, melted butter, and vanilla extract into a separate small bowl. Beat with a fork to combine. Pour the liquid mixture over the baking mix and stir with the fork until it is just mixed, and there are no visible traces of flour.

Heat a cast-iron skillet over medium-high heat. Place a pat of butter into the pan and swirl the pan to coat the cooking surface. Drop generous spoonfuls of batter 2 inches apart into the skillet. Your pancakes should be about 4 inches (10 cm) across: any larger and they won't cook evenly. Cook until the edges are set and air bubbles form on top, 2 to 3 minutes. Flip and cook 1 to 2 more minutes until the underside is golden. They can be served "to order" as they come off the griddle, or piled onto a platter and served family-style.

> **TECHNIQUE TIP** Sprinkle a few drops of water into the skillet to make sure the surface is properly heated before cooking the first batch of pancakes. If the water drops dance across the surface and quickly evaporate, then you're ready to get started.

Variation: Banana Pecan Pancakes

This is an easy and yummy way to upgrade basic buttermilk pancakes. After the batter is mixed, gently stir in $^2/_3$ cup (65 grams) chopped pecans and 1 peeled and chopped banana (200 grams) before cooking the pancakes.

MAKE AHEAD · V · 30 MINUTES OR LESS · PANTRY BASICS

GREEK YOGURT PANCAKES

I'd been successfully using yogurt as a substitute for eggs in baked goods for a few years before it ever occurred to me to try the same thing with pancakes. While I was at it, I figured I'd make them a little lighter, too, so I swapped in canola oil for the butter. One bite, and you won't miss a thing, at least not until you get to the bottom of the stack on your plate.

MAKES 10 PANCAKES

1$^{1}/_{3}$ cups (180 grams) Whole Grain Baking Mix (page 22)

$^{3}/_{4}$ cup (187 ml) milk

$^{1}/_{4}$ cup (54 grams) plain Greek yogurt

2 tablespoons (30 ml) canola oil

$^{1}/_{2}$ teaspoon (2.5 ml) vanilla extract

Add the baking mix to a medium bowl. Pour the milk, yogurt, oil, and vanilla extract into a separate small bowl. Beat with a fork to combine. Pour the liquid mixture over the dry ingredients and stir with the fork until just mixed, and there are no visible traces of flour.

Heat a cast-iron skillet over medium-high heat. Place a pat of butter into the pan and swirl the pan to coat the cooking surface. Drop generous spoonfuls of batter 2 inches apart into the skillet. Your pancakes should be about 4 inches (10 cm) across: any larger and they won't cook evenly. Cook until the edges are set and air bubbles form on top, 2 to 3 minutes. Flip and cook 1 to 2 more minutes until the underside is golden. They can be served "to order" as they come off the griddle, or piled onto a platter and served family style.

BASIC STEEL-CUT OATMEAL

Old-fashioned oats cook quickly, but they can't compete with the
nutty taste and tender bite of steel-cut oats. Put up a pot of them when you wake up, then set
about getting ready. You'll be rewarded with a filling breakfast to jumpstart your day by the time
you're ready to sit at the breakfast table.

SERVES 6 TO 8

1 cup steel-cut oats
Pinch of sea salt

Add 4 cups (1 L) of water to a 4-quart (3.5 L) pot. Bring to a boil. Add the oats and salt, stir, and
reduce the flame to low. Cook until the oats begin to thicken, the grains are slightly tender, and the
water has been mostly absorbed, 15 to 20 minutes. Turn off the heat, cover the pot, and let sit for 5
minutes before serving.

MAKE-AHEAD MEAL Cooked steel-cut oats reheat very well, so I like to make extra for
us to enjoy on busy weekday mornings. Store leftovers in a covered container. Spoon out
an individual portion into a bowl, adding a tablespoon or two of milk or water, then cover
loosely and microwave until heated through. One minute does the job in my 1000-watt
microwave.

VEGAN   MAKE AHEAD   GLUTEN-FREE   30 MINUTES OR LESS

STEEL-CUT OATS WITH CRÈME FRAÎCHE, RAISINS & PISTACHIOS

I love pairing oatmeal with a variety of toppings, and this combination is one of my favorites. If everyone in your family can't agree on pistachios and raisins, then set up a make-your-own oatmeal bar with bowls of assorted nuts and dried fruit. I have even been known to skip the nuts and fruit all together, and add a spoon of caramelized onions instead.

SERVES 2

1½ cups Basic Steel-Cut Oatmeal (page 53)

2 teaspoons (6 grams) packed light or dark brown sugar

4 tablespoons (40 grams) raisins

4 teaspoons (20 grams) crème fraîche

4 teaspoons (8 grams) chopped, shelled pistachios

Divide the cooked oats into two deep bowls. Sprinkle an even amount of sugar and raisins on top of each bowl of oatmeal. Add 2 teaspoons of crème fraîche to each bowl. Sprinkle the pistachios on top, and serve immediately.

HOMEMADE
with
Love

BAKED FRENCH TOAST

This recipe is one of those examples where you can use the same

ingredients with a different technique to create a game-changing meal. French toast is easy enough on its own—beat some eggs with milk and cinnamon, maybe even adding a bit of vanilla extract or beans for oomph before you dip the bread. I took that same idea but let the bread soak overnight to absorb the flavors even more. It's easier than regular French toast, and tastier, according to everyone at the table that morning.

SERVES 6 TO 8

1 loaf (475 grams) challah or egg bread

1 cup (250 ml) heavy whipping cream

1½ cups (375 ml) milk

4 large eggs

¼ cup (50 grams) granulated natural cane sugar

1 vanilla bean, split lengthwise and seeds scraped

2 teaspoons (6 grams) ground cinnamon

Grease the bottoms and sides of a 13-inch x 9-inch x 2-inch (33-cm x 22-cm x 5-cm) baking pan.

Cut the ends off the challah bread, and save them for making breadcrumbs or snacking. Cut the remaining loaf into 1-inch/2.5-cm-thick slices. Arrange the slices of bread in a single layer in the prepared pan. They do not need to fit tightly together like puzzle pieces in the pan. The bread will expand overnight, as it absorbs the liquid, and will fill the pan by the next morning.

In a large bowl, whisk together the cream, milk, eggs, sugar, vanilla bean seeds, and cinnamon until well blended. Pour over the bread in the pan. Use a rubber spatula to press the bread slices down to help soak up the milk mixture. Cover the pan with foil and place in the refrigerator 10 to 12 hours, or overnight.

The next morning, preheat the oven to 350ºF (180ºC). Leave the foil on the pan and bake the French toast for 30 minutes. Remove the foil and bake for another 20 minutes until it puffs up and the top is golden brown. Serve immediately.

DON'T WASTE A BITE This French toast is so good, you don't want even the smallest of leftover pieces going to waste. Wrap the slices individually in plastic wrap and store in the fridge for up to three days. To reheat, unwrap the slices and pop them into the toaster oven.

HOMEMADE
with
Love

MAKE
AHEAD

BROCCOLI RABE & FRESH RICOTTA FRITTATA

After months of nothing but root vegetables in the Northeast, spring signals the arrival of broccoli rabe at the farmers' market. I first made this dish for Easter Brunch two years ago, and it was a hit with my entire extended family. My mother taught me that briefly blanching the broccoli rabe takes away some of its bitterness. That Easter was also the first time my Uncle John tasted (and loved) my homemade ricotta (page 32). He's the head chef in his family, and I've always admired how much he loves being behind the stove. This simple frittata gave me a huge sense of accomplishment—my family is a tough crowd to please!

SERVES 8

1 small bunch (12 ounces/336 grams) broccoli rabe

12 large eggs

Fine sea salt and freshly ground black pepper

$^1/_2$ cup (100 grams) Creamy Homemade Ricotta (page 32)

1 tablespoon (15 ml) extra-virgin olive oil

Fill a 4-quart pot with water and bring to a boil. Fill a large bowl with ice water and set aside. Meanwhile, trim the tough bottoms off of the broccoli rabe. Add the broccoli rabe to the pot and cook until it starts to turn a bright green, about 2 minutes. Drain the broccoli rabe and plunge it into the bowl of ice-cold water to stop the cooking process. Wrap the broccoli rabe in a cloth towel or paper towels, and set it aside to let the towel absorb any excess water.

In a large bowl, beat the eggs well. Season them with salt and pepper to taste.

Preheat the oven to the broiler setting.

Add the olive oil to a 10-inch (25-cm) cast-iron skillet and place it over medium heat until the oil is shimmering. Add the broccoli rabe and pour in the eggs and let them cook undisturbed until the edges are set, about 1 minute. Slip a rubber spatula under the sides and tilt the pan to help the uncooked egg run underneath. Repeat this all around the edge of the pan until the top is wet but no longer runny.

Drop dollops of ricotta on top. Place the skillet under the broiler, and cook until the top puffs up and is golden and bubbly, 1 to 2 minutes, keeping a close eye so it doesn't burn.

Remove the pan from the oven, cut into 8 wedges, and serve immediately.

EGGS YOUR WAY

A perfectly cooked egg is one of the most satisfying meals, as far as I'm concerned. For the sake of space, I decided to stick with the three most popular preparations—scrambled, hard boiled, and poached. This last one is easier than most people think, so let's get cracking.

Perfect Poached Eggs

The first myth I want to dispel is that you need vinegar. You don't! Yes, I really did just say that. Vinegar gives a false sense of security when poaching eggs. Sure, it keeps the whites neat in the pot, but I've found it doesn't prevent the unwanted stringy parts from forming. I've read suggestions to strain the egg through a sieve into the boiling water, but when you're trying to cook quickly, and in my case, with two kids constantly interrupting, you need a quicker option. That is why I'm letting you in on the only secret you need to know for poaching eggs.

SERVES 1 TO 2

2 large eggs

Fill a 2-quart pot with water, leaving 1 inch of space from the rim. Bring the water to a boil.

Crack 1 egg into a small bowl or ramekin. Place a chopstick or a butter knife in the center of the pot, and stir vigorously to create a funnel effect (it should look like a mini tornado in the center of the pot). Gently slide the egg into the center, and watch as the funnel swirls the egg into shape. Reduce the flame to keep the water at a gentle bubble. Cook the egg for exactly 2 minutes. Using a slotted spoon, transfer the egg to a paper towel-lined plate to drain.

Repeat this process with the remaining egg. Serve immediately.

> **MAKE-AHEAD MEAL** Impress friends with poached eggs for brunch, but skip the stress of cooking them to order. Poached eggs can be prepared one to two days in advance, and stored in a tightly sealed container with just enough water to cover the eggs. When ready to serve, bring a small pot of water to a boil, slide the eggs in, and cook them until just heated through, about 30 seconds. Drain on a paper towel-lined plate for a few seconds before serving.

Fluffy Scrambled Eggs

Over the years, I've learned that one egg per person is too little, but two eggs are too much, so I've settled on three eggs as the perfect amount for two people. Use whatever number of eggs works for your family's appetite. Just stick to my low and slow method, and don't forget the butter—cooking spray just won't cut it for fluffy, creamy scrambled eggs.

SERVES 2

3 large eggs
Sea salt and freshly ground black pepper
2 teaspoons (9 grams) unsalted butter

Crack the eggs into a small bowl, season with salt and pepper to taste, and beat well.

Melt the butter in an 8-inch (20-cm) skillet over low heat. Add the eggs and cook them, undisturbed, for 1 minute. Continue cooking, this time stirring frequently with a wooden spoon, until the eggs are mostly cooked, but still wet-looking, about 4 to 5 minutes. Remove the pan from the heat, stir the eggs once more, then divide them between two dishes. Serve immediately.

Just Right Hard-Boiled Eggs

Hard-boiled eggs are a portable protein boost, and make for an easy breakfast on the go or an after-school snack paired with some crackers. If you purchase eggs from the farmers' market, they've likely been gathered the day before you bought them. Wait until later in the week to make your hard-boiled eggs, since older eggs are easier to peel.

MAKES 4

4 large eggs

Fill a 2-quart pot with water. Add the whole eggs to the pot and bring to a boil over medium heat. Once it reaches a boil, turn off the flame, cover the pot, and let it sit on the stove for 10 minutes.

Meanwhile, prepare a bowl of ice water.

Transfer the eggs to the bowl of water to stop the cooking process. Remove the eggs after 5 minutes, and crack and peel if eating immediately, or place in a tightly sealed container and store in the fridge for up to 3 days.

KALE, MUSHROOM & CHEDDAR CASSEROLE

The first time I made this casserole, it was actually a Sunday night,

giving us a new option for breakfast or dinner. I heated the leftovers for lunch the next day, making this one of my favorite kinds of recipes: the type that transcends meal times. So, why did I include it in the breakfast chapter? I love having friends over for brunch, but I also like sleeping in on the weekends—thankfully, my daughters are late risers, too. I can prep the casserole the night before, let it sit covered in the fridge while I sleep, and pop it into the oven an hour before company arrives.

SERVES 6

3 teaspoons (15 ml) extra-virgin olive oil, divided

1 bunch (7 ounces/200 grams) Tuscan kale, ribs removed and leaves thinly sliced

Sea salt and freshly ground black pepper

5 ounces (140 grams) cremini mushrooms, finely chopped

1 small yellow onion, thinly sliced

1/2 loaf (185 grams) ciabatta bread, cut into 1/8-inch/3-mm-thick slices

3 large eggs

1 1/2 cups (375 ml) milk

4 ounces (112 grams) Cheddar cheese, shredded

Preheat the oven to 350°F (180°C). Grease an 8-inch (20-cm) square baking dish and set aside.

Heat 2 teaspoons of the oil in a large skillet over medium heat. Add the kale and cook, stirring occasionally, until slightly wilted, 2 to 3 minutes. Add the mushrooms and onion to the skillet, and the remaining oil if the mixture looks too dry. Season with salt and pepper to taste. Turn the heat up to medium-high. Cook, stirring occasionally, until the mushrooms and onions are tender and lightly golden, 3 to 5 minutes. Remove from the heat and let cool 5 minutes.

In a medium bowl, beat the eggs and milk together until well mixed.

Use one third of the bread slices to cover the bottom of the prepared baking dish. Spread half of the kale mixture over the bread layer. Sprinkle one third of the cheese on top. Repeat this process to make one more layer. You will have the last third of the cheese remaining. Set it aside.

Pour the eggs over the casserole, and use a rubber spatula to gently press down the casserole layers to absorb the egg-milk mixture. Sprinkle the remaining cheese on top. Let the casserole sit for 15 minutes to further soak in the liquid, or cover tightly with foil and refrigerate overnight.

Cover with foil and bake for 30 minutes. Remove the foil and bake for 25 to 30 more minutes until the cheese is golden and bubbly. Let the casserole sit for 5 minutes before cutting into portions to serve.

6.

Soups,
SANDWICHES
& SALADS

THIS IS WHERE THE "I'LL TRY ANYTHING ONCE" FOOD writer admits that she survived on basically peanut butter and jelly sandwiches until middle school. True story—I was quite the picky eater, but let's keep that one hush-hush when my kids are in the room. Sure I still enjoy a good PB&J, especially when made with fresh strawberry jam (page 217), but I've come a long way in my eating habits. A comforting bowl of soup flecked with white beans, tiny ravioli and slivers of kale (page 73) or grilled Cheddar cheese, jazzed up with apple slices and pancetta (page 79), is more my speed these days.

When I was growing up, salad was served as a side, with basic lettuce and tomatoes as the usual suspects. Now I love eating them as main courses for lunch, or making a few different ones and serving them family-style for dinner. What I love most about making salads is the opportunity to combine a lot of flavors and textures, so there's something to keep you interested with every bite, as you'll see in two of my favorites here: Slow-Roasted Tomato & Fresh Mozzarella Panzanella (page 64) and Chickpea, Parmesan & Fennel Salad (page 69).

SLOW-ROASTED TOMATO & FRESH MOZZARELLA PANZANELLA

I remember my first panzanella as if it were yesterday. Mikey and I were on one of our vacations in Cape Cod, long before the girls were born. We had dinner on the deck at Adrian's in North Truro, and as the sun slowly dipped below the bay, the most amazing salad I've ever tasted was set before me. It was a trifecta of goodness: the company, the view, and the meal we were about to eat.

Since then, panzanella has been something I long for every summer when tomatoes are at their peak flavor. Life has changed so much since that quiet summer evening, but this salad proves that some changes can be good. Instead of using raw tomatoes, I took some liberties and used my Slow-Roasted Tomatoes (page 152). They add an intensity to this salad that I know Mikey would've loved as much as I do.

SERVES 2

1½ tablespoons (22 ml) extra-virgin olive oil

2 teaspoons (10 ml) apple cider vinegar

1 teaspoon (6 grams) honey

Sea salt flakes (I use Maldon) and freshly ground black pepper, to taste

2 cups (80 grams) Parmesan Skillet Croutons (page 35)

3 ounces (84 grams) fresh mozzarella, cubed

½ cup (127 grams) Slow-Roasted Tomatoes (page 152)

Handful of fresh basil leaves, torn

To make the dressing, whisk the oil, vinegar, honey, salt, and pepper together in a deep bowl. Adjust seasonings to taste. Add the croutons, mozzarella, tomatoes, and basil to the bowl, tossing well to combine. Let the salad sit for at least 5 minutes so the croutons can absorb the flavors, but no more than 15 minutes or they will get too soggy and lose their crunch. To serve, spoon the salad onto a platter or individual plates.

MAKE IT A MEAL If you have leftover roasted chicken, shred some and toss it into the salad for an easy one-bowl meal.

MEDITERRANEAN TUNA SALAD

I'm not a mayo girl, or at least I wasn't until I created the recipe on page 229. Before that, I needed a work-around for tuna salad—a Mikey favorite. He was skeptical about the vinaigrette dressing at first, but ended up loving the way it lightened up the salad. The olives add a briny, salty contrast and fresh chopped dill perks everything up, too. I'll admit he never was crazy about the inclusion of hard-boiled eggs, but marriage is all about compromise, right? Feel free to leave them out of your salad if you prefer.

I've strayed a little since the last time I made this sandwich for Mikey. Inspired by a craving for a Vietnamese bánh mì, I opted for fresh mint leaves over plain old lettuce as a garnish. My hunch was right, and while this is far from a bánh mì, the mint adds a refreshing burst to each bite.

SERVES 2

2 tablespoons (30 ml) extra-virgin olive oil

1 tablespoon (15 ml) red wine vinegar

1 teaspoon (2 grams) whole grain mustard

¹/₂ teaspoon (3 grams) honey

1 teaspoon (1 gram) chopped fresh dill

Sea salt and freshly ground black pepper

Two 5-ounce (140 grams) cans tuna (I use Wild Planet)

2 hard-boiled eggs (page 59), diced

¹/₄ cup (33 grams) pitted kalamata olives, chopped

4 slices of country white bread or baguette (optional)

6 fresh mint leaves, for garnish

Add the oil, vinegar, mustard, honey, and dill to a small bowl, and whisk to combine. Season with salt and pepper to taste.

Using your fingers, crumble the tuna into a separate deep bowl. Add the egg, olives, and dressing. Stir together to mix well. Spoon an even amount of the salad onto two slices of bread. Top each with three mint leaves, then top with the remaining bread. Serve immediately.

DAIRY-FREE

30 MINUTES OR LESS

RED GRAPE & DILL CHICKEN SALAD

I'm always looking for ways to use up leftover chicken, and this
chicken salad ranks high on my list. I love nibbling on little plates of food, so serving this
with some crackers on a little bread board is my idea of a perfect lunch. You can also make sandwiches with it, or simply add a scoop to a mixed green salad.

SERVES 2

1¼ cups (150 grams) chopped roasted chicken

10 red grapes, washed and cut into coins

1 teaspoon (1 gram) fresh chopped dill

3 tablespoons (56 grams) Homemade Mayonnaise (page 229)

Fine sea salt and freshly ground black pepper

Combine the chicken, grapes, dill, and mayonnaise in a deep bowl. Add salt and pepper to taste.
Using a rubber spatula, fold the mixture together until just combined. It can be made up to 1 day in
advance and stored in the fridge in a covered container, making it an easy lunch to pack for the
office, as Mikey often did.

GLUTEN-FREE   DAIRY-FREE   LEFT-OVERS   MAKE AHEAD

CHICKPEA, PARMESAN & FENNEL SALAD

I was a late bloomer when it came to loving fennel, but once I started
there was no stopping. This recipe originally began as a chickpea salad I made all the time. Then
one day, I spied the bulbs of fennel I'd just bought at the farmers' market and I wondered, "What
if…" Now, I often make this when I want a hearty vegetarian lunch.

SERVES 4

1 tablespoon (15 ml) apple cider vinegar

2 tablespoons (30 ml) extra-virgin olive oil

Freshly squeezed juice of 1 lemon

Sea salt and freshly ground black pepper

$^1/_2$ bulb of fennel, thinly sliced

$1^1/_2$ cups (420 grams) cooked chickpeas (A Pot of Beans, page 34)

$^1/_4$ cup (4 grams) fresh flat-leaf parsley, torn into pieces

$^1/_2$ cup (40 grams) shredded Parmesan cheese

$^1/_4$ cup (36 grams) Marcona almonds, coarsely chopped

In a large bowl, whisk together the vinegar, oil, and lemon juice until well mixed. Season the dressing with salt and pepper to taste. Add the fennel, chickpeas, parsley, and cheese to the bowl. Toss together to combine.

   To serve, spoon the salad onto a large platter, and sprinkle the almonds on top.

TIME SAVER You can prepare the salad up to an hour in advance, and let it sit at room temperature. The flavors have time to marinate this way, making it taste even better. Just wait to add the almonds until you're ready to serve it so they stay crunchy.

ZUCCHINI RIBBON SALAD WITH GRAPE TOMATOES & BASIL

If you've ever experienced the heat and humidity of a New York City summer, then you know cooking isn't the first thing on anyone's mind in July and August. That's when I go into my "no cook" mode, which offers great inspiration for looking at ingredients, especially seasonal produce, in a new light.

SERVES 2

1 large zucchini

¹/₂ pint (140 grams) grape tomatoes, cut in half

6 basil leaves, chopped

3 tablespoons (45 ml) Basic Vinaigrette (page 231)

Using a vegetable peeler, shave the zucchini into lengthwise strips. Add the zucchini, tomatoes, basil, and vinaigrette to a deep bowl and toss well to coat. Let the salad sit for 5 minutes before serving so the vinegar in the dressing can "cook" the zucchini a little.

30 MINUTES OR LESS · V · GLUTEN-FREE · EGG-FREE · DAIRY-FREE · MAKE AHEAD

ITALIAN LENTIL SOUP

I didn't have my first taste of lentil soup until well into adulthood, since my mom isn't a fan of legumes. Nowadays I'm making up for lost time, and I find myself putting up a pot once a week. My inspiration for this recipe came from a local Italian shop in my neighborhood called Caputo's. The soup has a peppery kick and chunks of vegetables that somehow manage to be incredibly tender while retaining their shape. A loaf of crusty bread is a must-have when serving this soup—my daughters love to dip slices in their bowls instead of using spoons to eat it.

SERVES 8 TO 10

1 tablespoon (15 ml) extra-virgin olive oil

3 medium carrots

1 medium yellow onion, diced

1 garlic clove, smashed

One (28-ounce/793-gram) can whole peeled tomatoes

1 medium potato, diced

Sea salt and freshly ground black pepper

2 cups (95 grams) brown lentils, picked over and rinsed

1 bay leaf

2 basil leaves, torn

Freshly grated Parmesan cheese, for garnish

Heat the olive oil in a 4-quart pot over medium heat. Add the carrots, onion, and garlic, and cook until the onion and garlic are lightly golden, 1 to 2 minutes. Add the tomatoes, one at a time, by squeezing them with your hands over the pot to roughly crush them. Pour in any juice from the can, too. Add the potatoes, 4 cups of water, salt, pepper, lentils, bay leaf, and basil. Adjust seasonings to taste. Bring to a boil, then cover and simmer on low heat for 45 minutes or until the lentils are tender. Remove and discard the bay leaf. Ladle into deep soup bowls and garnish with Parmesan cheese before serving.

FREEZE IT! Store leftovers in individual servings so they're easier to reheat. Use glass mason jars or, once the soup is cooled, you can use freezer-quality quart-sized bags. Seal the bag, removing as much air as possible, then lay the bag flat to maximize storage space in your freezer.

MAKE AHEAD · V · UNDER 1 HOUR · GLUTEN-FREE · EGG-FREE

CARROT-FENNEL SOUP

Carrots and ginger are a classic combination for soup, but I've never been one to follow the crowd. I knew from the start I wanted a carrot soup that would stand apart from all the others. As I browsed the market, I closed my eyes and just started sniffing bunches of vegetables. You all do that too, right? If not, try letting your nose guide you instead of your eyes the next time you go shopping. One licorice-laced whiff of fennel and I knew I had found another aromatic that would pair perfectly with carrots.

SERVES 4

2 teaspoons (10 ml) extra-virgin olive oil

1 pound (448 grams) carrots, peeled and cut into coins

1/2 bulb of fennel, thinly sliced

1 small yellow onion, cut into quarters

Sea salt and freshly ground black pepper

4 sprigs of fresh thyme, leaves removed and woody stems discarded

Freshly grated zest of 1 orange

1/4 teaspoon coriander

2 teaspoons (3 ml) heavy cream, for garnish (optional)

Heat the oil in a 2-quart pot over medium-high heat. Once the oil is shimmering, add the carrots, fennel, and onion. Cook, stirring occasionally, for 5 minutes, until the vegetables are fragrant and the onion becomes lightly golden. Season with salt and pepper to taste. Stir in the thyme leaves, orange zest, and coriander. Pour in 3 cups of water, stir well to combine, then raise the heat to high and bring to a boil. Reduce the heat to a simmer, and cook until the vegetables are very tender, about 20 minutes.

Remove the pot from the stove. Add the soup in batches to the bowl of a blender. Cover the blender, leaving the stopper on the blender cover cracked a bit to release steam, and hold a cloth towel over the top of it to avoid any splattering. Blend the soup into a smooth purée. Transfer to a clean pot. Once all the soup is puréed, heat it gently over low heat if it has cooled. Ladle the soup into 4 bowls, and swirl a 1/2 teaspoon of cream on top of each bowl, if desired, before serving.

TIME SAVER This soup is even better a day or two after it's been made. Store it in the fridge in a covered container, and reheat it gently over medium-low heat.

KALE, WHITE BEAN & RAVIOLI SOUP

I'm a year-round soup lover, even on the hottest of summer days.
My daughters did not inherit this trait, but they do love mini ravioli. So my trick to avoid their groans when I'm in a soup mood is to just add some tiny cheese ravioli. The little one loves kale, the big one not so much, but we all agree carrots rock, which is why I added them, too. Their love for beans can be fickle: sometimes they'll happily slurp them up in this soup, and other times they push them to the side. And that is what life is like even for a foodie mom—picky eaters are a rite of passage. As for the ingredients they don't like, it just means more of the good stuff for me.

SERVES 6

8 cups (64 ounces) vegetable stock (see also Homemade Vegetable Bouillon, page 24)
6 Lacinato (or Tuscan) kale leaves, ribs removed and leaves thinly sliced
3 carrots, peeled and sliced into 1/2-inch/0.5-cm-thick coins
1/2-inch (1.5 cm) piece rind of Parmesan cheese
2 cups (420 grams) cooked small white beans (or one 15-ounce can, drained)
8 ounces (784 grams) frozen mini ravioli, prepared according to package directions
Freshly ground black pepper

Combine the stock, kale, carrots, and Parmesan rind in a large pot. Bring to a boil over medium-high heat, then reduce the heat to a simmer and let cook for 20 minutes. Add the beans and cook the soup for 5 to 10 more minutes until the carrots and kale are tender.

Remove and discard the cheese rind. Stir in the cooked ravioli and cook for 1 minute until the pasta is heated through. Ladle into deep soup bowls and season with black pepper to taste before serving.

V **MAKE AHEAD**

SECRET INGREDIENT FRENCH ONION SOUP

Vegetarian versions of this classic soup usually fall short on flavor—but not here. One day I wondered what would happen if I added some molasses to the mix. The result is a soup with as much depth of flavor as its beef stock counterpart. And talk about quick and easy—the stock is made right in the pot, picking up all the flavors from the caramelized bits of onion.

SERVES 4

4 tablespoons (56 grams) unsalted butter

4 large yellow onions, sliced

1 bay leaf

Fine sea salt and freshly ground black pepper

1 garlic clove, crushed

1 tablespoon (15 ml) sherry vinegar

1 tablespoon (15 ml) molasses

Four 1-inch/2.5-cm-thick slices of baguette, toasted

4 ounces (112 grams) Swiss or Gruyere cheese, shredded

Melt the butter in a 6-quart stockpot over medium-high heat. Add the onions and bay leaf and season with salt and pepper to taste. Stir to coat well. Cook, stirring occasionally, until the onions begin to soften and become golden, about 15 minutes. Cover the pot and reduce the heat to medium-low. Cover and cook until the onions are very soft and browned, about 20 more minutes.

Remove and discard the bay leaf. Stir, scraping up browned bits at the bottom of the pot. Raise the heat back to medium-high and slowly pour in 2½ cups (675 ml) water. Add the garlic clove, sherry vinegar, and molasses, and bring to a boil. Reduce the heat to low, so the soup gently bubbles, and cook for 10 more minutes. Taste and season the soup with additional salt and pepper, if necessary.

Preheat the broiler with the oven rack just under the broiler element. Evenly ladle the soup into 4 oven-safe bowls. Place one slice of toasted baguette on top of each serving of soup. Sprinkle the cheese evenly on top and place on a rimmed baking sheet. Place in the oven and cook until the cheese becomes golden and bubbly, 2 to 3 minutes.

GLUTEN-FREE FRIENDLY Swap in toasted slices of your favorite gluten-free bread, and everyone can enjoy this soup.

RIBOLLITA

"Reboiled" doesn't sound appealing for a recipe name, but that's exactly what *ribollita* means in Italian. The origins of this Tuscan soup were a thrifty, tasty way to give new life to leftovers. Beans and a medley of vegetables simmer with thick slices of bread that melt into the stock, creating a thick, hearty, one-bowl meal. Recipes vary, and many call for a combination of leafy greens, but I decided to keep my version simple and use my favorite: Lacinato kale. Feel free to substitute an equal amount of cabbage, Swiss chard, or other variety of kale, depending on what you can easily find at the market.

SERVES 6 TO 8

4 slices (46 grams) bacon, diced

3 large carrots, peeled and sliced into coins

3 ribs celery, diced

1 medium yellow onion, diced

2 garlic cloves, crushed

4 cups (1000 ml) vegetable stock (see also Homemade Vegetable Bouillon, page 24)

2-inch (5-cm) piece Parmesan rind (116g)

1 (14-ounce/396-gram) can diced tomatoes, undrained

1³/₄ cups (15 ounces) cooked white beans, such as cannellini or navy (page 34)

1 bunch (176 grams) Lacinato kale or any other hearty fresh greens (see recipe headnote)

Two 1-inch/2.5-cm-thick slices crusty country-style bread, torn into bite-size pieces

Freshly ground black pepper

In a 4-quart pot over medium-high heat, cook the bacon until crisp. Using a slotted spoon, transfer the bacon to a paper towel-lined plate to drain.

Add the carrots, celery, onion, and garlic to the bacon drippings in the pan. Reduce the heat to medium, and cook until the vegetables are slightly softened, 5 to 7 minutes.

Add the vegetable stock, cheese rind, diced tomatoes, and cooked bacon to the pot. Bring the soup to a boil, then reduce the heat to a gentle simmer. Cook for 10 minutes.

Add the beans and kale, cover the pot, and cook for 10 more minutes. Stir in the bread, season with pepper to taste, and let cook, uncovered, for 5 more minutes. Remove from the heat and let the soup "rest" for 5 minutes before serving, so the bread can continue to soak up the stock. Remove and discard the cheese rind.

Ladle into deep soup bowls to serve.

EASY VEGETARIAN Just omit the bacon, and use 2 teaspoons of extra-virgin olive oil to sauté the vegetables.

ROASTED TOMATO SOUP

I should start by saying that I wasn't a fan of tomato soup before making
this one. I always felt that anything of the puréed tomato variety was best used to coat pasta, not
served straight up in a bowl with a spoon. I now realize how incredibly silly that is, and am here to
say if you don't like tomato soup, then give this one a try. The cloves add a warm, spicy kick that
makes it worthy of wiping the bowl clean with a chunk of bread.

SERVES 4

1 (28-ounce/793-gram) can peeled whole tomatoes

Sea salt and freshly ground black pepper

1 tablespoon (10 grams) packed dark brown sugar

$^1\!/_2$ teaspoon (1 gram) ground cloves

2 teaspoons (10 ml) extra-virgin olive oil, plus more as needed for drizzling

1 cup (250 ml) vegetable stock (see also Homemade Bouillon, page 24)

$^1\!/_4$ cup (62 ml) heavy whipping cream

Parmesan Skillet Croutons, for garnish (page 35)

Preheat the oven to 300°F (150°C). Line a baking sheet with heavy-duty foil.

Drain the tomatoes, saving the juices for later in preparing the soup (you should have about 1$^1\!/_2$
cups reserved). Slice the tomatoes in half and place them cut-side up on the prepared baking sheet.

In a small bowl, use a fork to mix together the salt, pepper, brown sugar, and cloves. Adjust seasonings to taste. Evenly sprinkle the mixture over the tomatoes. Drizzle the olive oil over the tomatoes and roast for 1 hour until they are collapsed. Remove the tray from the oven and let the
tomatoes cool for 10 minutes.

Transfer the cooled tomatoes to a blender. Add the vegetable stock and reserved tomato juice
and blend until smooth. You may need to do this in two batches, depending on the size and speed
of your blender.

Pour the soup into a 2-quart pot and heat until warmed, but not boiling. Stir in the cream and
cook for another minute. Ladle the soup into bowls, and garnish with the croutons before serving.

VEGAN-FRIENDLY While I love to finish this with a bit of cream, you can omit it altogether (and the croutons, too) for a healthier vegan, gluten-free version that's an equally
delicious and comforting bowl of soup.

APPLE, CHEDDAR & PANCETTA PANINI

Mikey was a kid at heart, and what kid doesn't love a good grilled cheese sandwich? This is my way of bringing that kid classic into adulthood, making it a more grown-up panini. Here, I've gussied it up with pancetta, an Italian-style bacon. The tart sweetness of the apple blends perfectly with the crispy saltiness of the pancetta. When I first made this sandwich for Mikey, he bit in, closed his eyes, and let out a big sigh. I knew I'd hit a homerun.

SERVES 4

8 thin slices pancetta
8 thick slices country bread
Whole grain mustard (page 227), for spreading
8 slices Cheddar cheese
1 tart green apple, thinly sliced (I like Granny Smith)
1 tablespoon (14 grams) unsalted butter

Preheat a skillet over medium heat. Cook the pancetta until it's nicely browned and crisp. Remove from the skillet and set on a paper towel-lined dish to drain.

Lay 4 pieces of bread on a counter or cutting board. Spread a thin layer of mustard on each slice. Then top with one slice of cheese. Layer 2 to 3 slices of apple on top, then add 2 slices of cooked pancetta on top of that. Lay another slice of cheese over the pancetta, and finish assembling the sandwiches by adding a slice of bread on top.

Heat a cast-iron skillet over medium heat. Melt half of the butter in the pan. Place two sandwiches in the skillet and cook until the bottom of the sandwiches are golden and the cheese is beginning to melt, 2 to 3 minutes. Using a spatula, flip the sandwiches over, weigh them down with a heavy-bottomed pot, and cook on the remaining side until it, too, is golden and the cheese is now fully melted, about 2 more minutes. Repeat with the remaining two sandwiches. Serve immediately.

PRESSED FOR TIME? You can assemble the sandwiches in the morning, wrap them in parchment paper so the bread doesn't get soggy, and store them in the fridge. When you get home, all you need to do is cook them for a quick dinner. Make it a meal by adding a side salad.

79
SOUPS,
SAND
WICHES&
SALADS

TOMATO JAM, MOZZARELLA & SPINACH PANINI

One day I found myself with a hankering for a Caprese sandwich, but tomato season was over, and there wasn't a basil leaf to be found in the fridge. I did have some leftover spinach, though, and Sweet & Savory Tomato Jam (page 216) in the pantry, which meant I could put a wintery spin on my favorite summertime sandwich.

SERVES 2

1 teaspoon (5 ml) extra-virgin olive oil, plus more for drizzling

1 shallot, thinly sliced

1 cup (42 grams) packed baby spinach, well rinsed and dried

4 slices country or white Pullman bread

3 tablespoons (57 grams) Sweet and Savory Tomato Jam (page 216)

3 ounces (84 grams) fresh mozzarella, thinly sliced

Heat the olive oil in a small nonstick skillet over medium-low heat. Add the shallot and cook until it's fragrant, about 1 minute. Add the spinach and cook until it's wilted, 1 to 2 minutes. Remove from the heat and set aside.

Preheat a cast-iron skillet over medium.

Meanwhile, arrange 2 slices of bread on a countertop or cutting board. Slather an equal amount of tomato jam on each slice. Top with equal amounts of mozzarella. Arrange equal amounts of spinach on top of the cheese. Top with the remaining slices of bread.

Drizzle a bit of olive oil in the skillet. Place the sandwiches in the skillet and use a heavy-bottomed pot to weigh them down. Cook until the undersides are nicely browned, then turn and place the heavy-bottomed pot back on top of the sandwiches. Continue to cook until they are golden on the other side and the cheese is melted. Serve immediately.

7.

Pasta, BEANS & GRAINS

*P*ASTA WAS A STAPLE WHEN I WAS GROWING UP. IT continues to be an A-list star in my own kitchen, except now I make my own fresh pasta as often as possible—the Linguine with White Clam Sauce holds a very special place in my heart since it was Mikey's specialty (keep an eye out for it in the Seafood chapter, page 121).

As we began eating less meat, beans started playing a bigger role in our meals, too. I put up a pot of one or two types of homemade beans on Mondays to use throughout the week. Sometimes that means adding them to pasta, as in the Orecchiette with Lentils & Tomatoes (page 86), and other times they get top billing in dishes like my Smoky Corn & Bean "Chili" (page 98).

HOMEMADE EGG PASTA

When I met Mikey eighteen years ago, I found a hand-cranked pasta

maker sitting amongst the pots and pans in his kitchen cupboard. I'm not sure he ever made pasta before we met, but once I took up residence in his home, it got a regular workout. Everyone should try their hand at homemade pasta at least once, for two reasons—to see how easy it really is to make, and to experience just how amazing it tastes. I bet once you try it, you'll be hooked. Another bonus: fresh pasta cooks quickly in boiling water, 2 to 5 minutes, depending on the thickness.

SERVES 6 TO 8

1¹/₂ cups (220 grams) unbleached all-purpose flour

¹/₂ cup (80 grams) durum semolina flour, plus more for sprinkling

2 large eggs, at room temperature

¹/₂ teaspoon (3 grams) fine sea salt

Add the flours to a deep glass or metal bowl. Whisk to combine. Using a spoon, make a "well" in the center of the flour, leaving a thin layer of flour at the bottom of it. Add the eggs and salt. Using a fork, stir the mixture in a quick circular motion, starting with small circles and working your way outwards, until it forms a sticky dough. All the flour will not mix in, and that's just fine.

Scoop the dough out of the bowl and place it on a clean counter. Pour the remaining flour into a strainer and shake it over the pasta dough. Discard any large bits of dough left inside the strainer (do not be tempted to press it into your nice smooth dough).

Knead the dough, working in as much of the remaining flour as needed, until it becomes smooth, but not dry. Again, you may not need to work in all the flour. Wrap the dough in plastic and let it rest for at least 20 minutes and up to 2 hours at room temperature.

When ready to roll out the dough, divide it into 4 equal pieces. Following the directions on your pasta machine, roll it into thin sheets. Once the sheets are rolled, the pasta can then be used as lasagna noodles, cut into fettuccine or angel hair, or filled with cheese to make ravioli—you name it, really. Cut pasta should be sprinkled lightly with semolina flour to prevent the strands from sticking together until ready to cook.

> **TRICKS OF THE TRADE** I add a bit of semolina flour to my dough to help give it elasticity. The other secret to smooth, easy-to-work pasta dough is rest. The dough needs a break from all that hard work to let the glutens relax before a roll through the pasta machine: as little as 20 minutes is fine, or up to two hours. Lastly, room-temperature eggs are crucial to allow for proper absorption of the wet and dry ingredients, so plan accordingly.

ORECCHIETTE WITH LENTILS & TOMATOES

I love pasta in all sorts of shapes, but if I had to pick a favorite, it might very well be orecchiette. Sauces cling to the ridges, and in this case the lentils nestle perfectly in the center of this little ear-shaped pasta. Caputo's, an Italian market near my house, sells a hand-made rustic pasta with a hearty, chewy, toothsome quality that compliments this dish, instead of the pasta merely being a vehicle for the sauce.

SERVES 4

8 ounces (226 grams) uncooked orecchiette pasta

2 teaspoons (10 ml) extra-virgin olive oil

2 garlic cloves, thinly sliced

4 ripe plum tomatoes, seeded and diced

Fine sea salt and freshly ground black pepper

$1/4$ cup (62 ml) white wine

$1/3$ cup (65 grams) lentils, picked over and rinsed

$1/2$ cup (28 grams) grated Parmesan cheese

Chopped fresh parsley, for serving

Prepare the pasta al dente according to the package directions, reserving $1/4$ cup of the cooking water.

Meanwhile, heat the oil in a deep skillet over medium-high heat until it's shimmering. Add the garlic and cook until it's lightly golden and fragrant, 1 to 2 minutes. Add the tomatoes and season with salt and pepper to taste. Cook, stirring occasionally, until the tomatoes collapse slightly and release some of their juices, 2 to 3 minutes. Pour in the wine and $3/4$ (190 ml) cup of water. Add the lentils, stir, and bring the sauce to a boil. Reduce the heat to medium-low so bubbles pop gently to the surface, and cook until the lentils are tender, about 15 minutes. Gradually add the reserved pasta water to the pan if the sauce gets too dry before the lentils are cooked through (it should be thick enough so it clings to the pasta, but not soupy).

Add the pasta to the skillet, tossing to coat it well. Sprinkle the cheese on top, and toss again. Divide the pasta among four deep bowls and serve garnished with parsley.

FETTUCCINE WITH BASIL-WALNUT PESTO

Traditional pesto recipes use pine nuts, but they're quite expensive— around $30 per pound. After years of experimenting with various pesto recipes made from other herb and nut combinations, I decided it was time to revisit my basil pesto. I swapped in walnuts since they're more economical, averaging $10 per pound. When it came time for the taste test, I discovered I love basil pesto even more when made this way.

SERVES 4

12 ounces (336 grams) uncooked fettuccine

3/4 cup (35 grams) packed fresh basil leaves

Handful of flat-leaf parsley, leaves and stems

1 garlic clove, thinly sliced

4 tablespoons (112 grams) unsalted butter, at room temperature

1/4 cup (25 grams) shelled walnuts, toasted

1/4 cup (18 grams) freshly grated Parmesan cheese, plus more for serving

Sea salt and freshly ground black pepper

1/4 cup (62 ml) extra-virgin olive oil

Prepare the fettuccine according to the package directions.

Meanwhile, add the basil and parsley to a food processor. Pulse them 2 to 3 times to roughly chop the herbs. Add the garlic, butter, walnuts, cheese, and season with salt and pepper. Adjust seasonings to taste. Process until it forms a paste, about 30 seconds, then begin slowly drizzling the olive oil in through the feed tube. Continue to process the mixture until it begins becomes creamy and sauce-like.

At this point, the pesto can simply be tossed with the hot pasta, but heating it up intensifies the flavor. If desired, pour the pesto into the pot you used to cook the pasta. Place it over medium-low heat until it is warmed but not boiling. Add the cooked pasta to the pot and toss it vigorously to coat every strand. Divide among four deep serving bowls, and, if desired, top with Parmesan cheese before serving.

MAKE AHEAD The pesto can be made up to two weeks in advance, and stored in the fridge until ready to use. It will harden up, like butter, making it easy to scoop out the amount you need (it's also perfect for spreading on toasted baguette and topping with the Slow Roasted Tomatoes on page 152 and fresh mozzarella).

30 MINUTES OR LESS   FF   V   MAKE AHEAD

HOMEMADE MANICOTTI

Purists may argue that manicotti are an Italian-American invention and not from the homeland, but a little detective work shows it has some authentic roots. *Crespelle alla Fiorentina* is a dish from Florence, Italy. In that recipe, the "pasta" crêpes are filled with a spinach and ricotta cheese filling, then topped with a thin layer of *balsamella* (more commonly known by its French name, béchamel) sauce followed by a layer of tomato sauce. Sounds a bit familiar, right? Perhaps the Italian-American manicotti made with a simple ricotta cheese filling sans spinach and only one sauce instead of two simply evolved while adjusting to life in a new land.

MAKES 8 TO 10 FILLED PASTA CREPES

PASTA CRÊPES

1 large egg

1 cup (140 grams) unbleached all-purpose flour

1/4 teaspoon (2 grams) fine sea salt

1 1/2 cups (375 ml) milk, plus more as needed to thin the batter

Canola oil, for lightly greasing the pan

2 cups (450 grams) 20-Minute Marinara Sauce (page 27)

RICOTTA FILLING

16 ounces (453 grams) Creamy Homemade Ricotta (page 32)

1 large egg, lightly beaten

Small handful of fresh flat-leaf parsley, chopped

1/4 cup (18 grams) freshly grated Pecorino Romano cheese

Sea salt and freshly ground black pepper

FINISHING

1/4 cup (18 grams) grated Pecorino Romano cheese

For the pasta crêpes: combine the egg, flour, salt, and milk in the bowl of a blender. Blend until the batter is a very thin, pourable consistency, adding additional milk if necessary, 1 teaspoon (1.5 ml) at a time.

Heat an 8-inch (20 cm) crepe pan over medium-low heat. Brush the pan lightly with oil. Hold the pan at an angle, and quickly swirl it as you pour in just enough batter to coat the bottom. Cook about 45 seconds, until the edges look slighty crisp and the top begins to look dry. Gently slip an offset spatula underneath the crêpe, flip, and cook for 15 more seconds. The first couple will be

HOMEMADE
with
Love

sacrificial until you get the hang of swirling the pan. Transfer to a flat dish or tray. Repeat with the remaining batter.

Preheat the oven to 350°F (180°C).

Spread ½ cup (112 grams) of marinara sauce onto the bottom of a 9-inch by 13-inch (22-cm x 33-cm) casserole dish. To make the filling, add the ricotta, egg, parsley, Pecorino, and salt and pepper to a medium bowl and stir with a fork to combine. Adjust seasonings to taste.

Lay pasta crêpes on a flat surface and spoon an even amount of the filling in a long strip down the center of each one. Roll crêpes closed, and place seam-side down into the casserole dish. Pour the remaining sauce evenly over the filled crepes. Sprinkle the remaining grated cheese on top and bake for 20 minutes, until golden and bubbly. Let the manicotti sit for 2 minutes before serving.

TOOLS OF THE TRADE Surprisingly, a good crêpe pan is a relatively inexpensive investment—around $20 at a kitchen store like Sur La Table. If you have trouble finding one, an 8-inch (20-cm) nonstick skillet works well, too.

MAKE AHEAD The cooked crêpes can be stored in a plastic zip-top bag in the refrigerator for up to a week, or frozen for up to three months (place a piece of waxed paper between each crepe to prevent them from sticking). The assembled manicotti can be stored in a covered casserole dish in the refrigerator overnight—just top with the sauce and pop it in the oven come dinnertime.

UNDER 1 HOUR MAKE AHEAD V FF

MUSHROOM BOLOGNESE

When Mikey and I first met, he was living in Astoria, Queens and we often went to an Italian restaurant called Penna under the "el" on Broadway and 31st Street. When we first tasted their penne with mushroom sauce, we fell in love with the finely minced bits of mushroom that clung to each piece of pasta. We assumed this was how mushroom sauce was prepared in all Italian-American joints, only to be sorely disappointed—most just sauté sliced mushrooms and add them to marinara sauce.

Flash forward ten years, and one kid later. Getting Isabella to eat mushrooms used to be a nearly impossible feat. She does like Bolognese sauce, though, and it got me thinking about that mushroom sauce Mikey and I had all those years before. I decided to mince some white button mushrooms—they're milder in flavor than other types—and swap them in for the ground beef. It finally made a mushroom eater of her, and, in a sweet way, bridged our past with our present.

SERVES 4

1 tablespoon (15 ml) extra-virgin olive oil

10 ounces (280 grams) white button mushrooms, wiped cleaned and chopped very fine

1 medium onion, finely chopped

Sea salt and freshly ground black pepper

¼ cup (62 ml) red wine

2 cups (450 grams) 20-Minute Marinara Sauce (page 27)

8 ounces (226 grams) uncooked spaghetti

Freshly grated Parmesan cheese, for serving (optional)

Heat the olive oil in a skillet over medium-high heat. Add the mushrooms and onions and cook until both are golden, 5 to 7 minutes. Season with salt and pepper to taste.

Add the red wine, and bring it to a boil. Reduce the heat to a simmer, and cook until the wine is reduced by half, 3 to 4 minutes.

Meanwhile, set a large pot of water over high-heat and bring to a boil.

Stir in the marinara, and bring the sauce back to a boil. Lower the flame to a simmer and cook for 10 more minutes until the sauce has reduced slightly. Right about now is a good time to get your dry pasta into the pot of boiling water.

Cook and drain the pasta, and add it to the skillet with the sauce. Toss well. Divide the pasta into four deep serving bowls. Serve with the grated Parmesan, if desired.

VEGAN FRIENDLY · EGG-FREE · FF · 30 MINUTES OR LESS

LENTIL RICOTTA "MEATBALLS"

Growing up in an Italian family, meatballs were a Sunday dinner staple.
This recipe came about because I was determined to make a less expensive, tasty vegetarian version to stretch my grocery budget. I don't know why I thought puréed lentils were the answer, but boy am I glad I gave them a try.

MAKES ABOUT 18 MEATBALLS

2 cups (400 grams) cooked lentils, puréed

2 large eggs, lightly beaten

$2/3$ cup (85 grams) plain breadcrumbs (see sidebar)

$1/4$ cup fresh (58 grams) Creamy Homemade Ricotta (page 32)

$1/4$ cup (18 grams) grated Pecorino Romano cheese

$1^1/2$ teaspoons (3 grams) chopped fresh flat-leaf parsley

Sea salt and freshly ground black pepper

Canola oil, for frying

20-Minute Marinara sauce (optional) (page 27)

Combine the lentils, eggs, breadcrumbs, ricotta, Pecorino, parsley, and salt and pepper to taste in a deep bowl. Mix very well, using your hands or a wooden spoon. Cover and refrigerate for at least 2 hours, or overnight.

When ready to cook, shape the mixture into $1^1/2$-inch (3.75-cm) balls.

Add $1/2$ inch (1.25 cm) of oil to a nonstick skillet. Heat over a medium flame until the oil is shimmering. Add the shaped meatballs to the pan in batches, making sure not to overcrowd the pan, and cook until they are browned all around, turning only once. Transfer to a paper towel-lined plate and let the excess oil drain. Add the cooked meatballs to simmering marinara sauce if serving immediately and simmer for an hour to soak up the sauce. (If you're pressed for time, half an hour will do.) Store the cooked meatballs in a tightly covered container for up to 3 days.

GLUTEN-FREE FRIENDLY Swap in stale gluten-free bread to make your own breadcrumbs (see the Technique Tip below) and everyone can enjoy this recipe.

TECHNIQUE TIP Imagine making money by selling stale bread—that's what bakeries and big companies do all the time! Save those stray pieces left from the previous night's dinner in a paper bag. As they dry out, give them a quick pulse in the food processor and you'll always have free homemade breadcrumbs on hand.

VEGETABLE NOODLE STIR FRY

Like fried rice (page 96), this dish works best with leftover cooked noodles. I usually cook a double batch of spaghetti and leave half plain so I'll have part of the prep work done for quick meals on busy weeknights, which are par for the course when you enter parenthood. The kids have sensitive palates as far as spices go, so I keep it on the mild side for them and a have bottle of Sriracha sauce on hand for me when I want a blast of heat on my noodles.

SERVES 4

1 garlic clove

1-inch (2.5-cm) piece of fresh ginger, peeled

Pinch of fine sea salt

2 teaspoons (10 ml) sesame oil

3 tablespoons Nama Shoyu (unpasteurized soy sauce)

¼ teaspoon granulated natural cane sugar

1 tablespoon (15 ml) olive oil

1 small onion, thinly sliced

3 large white mushrooms, thinly sliced

1 small bunch (about 112 grams) broccoli, florets cut into small pieces—save the stalks for another use (page 160)

½ of a red bell pepper, thinly sliced

2 carrots, peeled and thinly sliced on the diagonal

½ cup (52 grams) frozen peas

12 ounces (340 grams) cold leftover cooked spaghetti

Freshly ground black pepper

Handful of chopped scallions, green part only, for garnish

On a cutting board, coarsely chop the garlic and ginger. Sprinkle the salt on top and continue chopping until it forms a paste. Set aside.

In a small bowl, whisk together the sesame oil, Shoyu sauce, and sugar. Set aside.

Heat a wok over medium-high heat. Add the oil and let it heat until shimmering, about 30 seconds. Add the onions and stir quickly, using a wooden or metal spatula, until the onions are golden, about 1 minute. Add the mushrooms and, stirring continuously, cook them until they've released their liquid and are lightly browned, about 2 minutes. Add the garlic-ginger paste to the wok and stir vigorously. Add the broccoli, bell pepper, and carrots to the wok. Cook, stirring vigorously, for 30 seconds, then cover the wok and let the vegetables cook until they're al dente, 2 to 3 minutes.

Add the peas to the wok, along with the spaghetti and the sesame oil-Nama Shoyu sauce mixture. Toss well to combine, and continue cooking until the noodles and peas are heated through, 1 to 2 more minutes. Season with black pepper to taste and garnish with the scallions before serving.

READY, SET, COOK! Speed is key in stir-fry cooking, so prepping *all* your ingredients *before* starting to cook is essential. Once the ingredients are prepped, the active cooking time for most dishes is just a matter of minutes.

30 MINUTES OR LESS · VEGAN

VEGETABLE FRIED RICE

There's no shortage of Chinese takeout in New York City, but if you're looking for *good* takeout, then that's a different story. Instead of settling for greasy rice with overcooked vegetables, I took matters into my own hands, literally, and came up with a recipe that's closer in taste to the fried rice Mikey and I used to enjoy at his favorite restaurant down on the Bowery in Chinatown.

SERVES 4 TO 6

4 teaspoons (20 ml) soy sauce

1 teaspoon (5 ml) oyster sauce

1 teaspoon (5 ml) sesame oil

1 tablespoon (15 ml) canola oil, divided, plus more as needed

1 small onion, chopped

2 carrots, diced

6 cremini mushrooms (also called baby bella), sliced

1 large egg, lightly beaten

¼ cup (26 grams) frozen peas

4 cups (780 grams) leftover cold brown rice

Sea salt and freshly ground black pepper

3 scallions, chopped

In a small bowl, whisk together the soy sauce, oyster sauce, and sesame oil. Set aside.

Heat 1 teaspoon of the canola oil in a wok over medium-high heat. Add the onion, carrots, and mushrooms and cook until the onion and mushrooms are golden, 2 to 3 minutes. Push the vegetables to the outer sides of wok or skillet and heat another teaspoon of oil over medium-heat. Add the egg and use a chopstick or fork to scramble it.

Add the peas, rice, and remaining oil to the wok. Stir it vigorously to mix well and break up any large clumps of rice, adding more oil, 1 teaspoon at a time, if the rice sticks to the wok. Pour the reserved soy sauce mixture over the rice and stir well to coat. Season with salt and pepper to taste.

Spoon the rice onto a platter and scatter the scallions on top to serve. If you're lucky enough to have any leftovers, this is great for packing in lunchboxes—for both kids *and* adults.

EASY VEGETARIAN Just omit the oyster sauce, and add extra soy sauce in its place.

SLOW-ROASTED BEET, FETA & FARRO SALAD

Is it crazy to admit that a salad can make me squeal with excitement?
Well, this one does. I love the nutty, chewy bits of farro studded with earthy wedges of roasted beets. The feta cheese and the fresh chopped oregano add some Mediterranean flair to the salad.

SERVES 4

3 medium-sized beets, peeled and cut in half

$^1/_4$ cup (62 ml) plus 3 tablespoons (45 ml) extra-virgin olive oil, divided

Sea salt and freshly ground black pepper

3 tablespoons (45 ml) apple cider vinegar

1 teaspoon (5 ml) honey

1 cup (200 grams) uncooked semi-pearled farro, prepared according to the package directions and cooled

2 ounces (56 grams) feta cheese, crumbled

1 tablespoon (12 grams) fresh chopped oregano

Preheat the oven to 300°F (150°C).

Place the beets, cut-side down, in an 8-inch (20-cm) square baking dish. Drizzle $^1/_4$ cup (62 ml) of the olive oil over them, and season with salt and pepper to taste. Bake them until very tender when pierced with a fork, about 2 hours. Remove the beets from the oven and let them cool slightly. Once cooled, cut each half into three wedges.

To make the dressing, whisk the remaining olive oil with the vinegar and honey in a deep bowl. Season with salt and pepper to taste. Add the farro to the bowl, and stir well to combine. Fold in the feta cheese and oregano. Spoon the salad onto a platter and scatter the beets on top to serve.

MAKE AHEAD The salad itself should be assembled and eaten as soon as it's made, but you can prepare the individual components in advance. Both the beets and the farro can be cooked up to two days in advance and stored in the fridge. The dressing can be made up to one week in advance and stored in a jar in the fridge, too. When ready to serve, just assemble the salad as noted in the directions.

EASY VEGAN Swap in agave nectar for the honey and omit the feta cheese.

SMOKY CORN & BEAN "CHILI"

I've put chili in quotation marks to keep Texan purists at bay—real chili isn't supposed to have beans and is made with chunks of beef. Now that we've got that matter of authenticity settled, let's talk about this dish's merits. It's quick-cooking, ready in less than 30 minutes, and can be made ahead and reheated for an even faster weeknight dinner. My girls love it served over rice and, frankly, I'm in agreement.

MAKES 4 TO 6 SERVINGS

2 ounces (84 grams) smoked bacon, diced

1 small onion, diced

1 to 2 teaspoons extra-virgin olive oil, or as needed

1½ cups (198 grams) frozen corn kernels, not thawed

1 cup (250 grams) home-canned or jarred salsa (not fresh salsa)

2 cups pinto beans

2 teaspoons (2 grams) fresh chopped cilantro

Shredded Cheddar cheese, for serving (optional)

Heat a 3-quart pot over medium heat. Add the bacon and cook until crisp. Use a slotted spoon to transfer the bacon to a small bowl or plate.

Add the onion to the pot and cook until slightly tender, 1 to 2 minutes. You might need to add 1 to 2 teaspoons of olive oil to the pan, depending on how much grease the bacon released during cooking: the onions should not stick to the pan. Add the frozen corn and salsa, stirring to mix well. Bring the chili to a gentle boil. Add the beans and reduce the heat to a simmer, with a few bubbles popping to the surface. Cook for 10 more minutes. Ladle the chili into deep serving bowls, and garnish with the cilantro and Cheddar cheese, if desired, before serving.

> **EASY VEGETARIAN** Just skip the bacon and add a little chipotle powder for an extra kick of spice and smoky flavor. To make it vegan, leave out the Cheddar cheese.

8.

Meaty MAINS

I STARTED BUYING MY BEEF AND CHICKEN FROM Grazin' Angus Acres at the farmers' market four years ago, and have since become good friends with the family that runs the farm up in Ghent, New York. I've sent well wishes for the birth of two of their grandchildren and felt blessed myself when their son's tour of duty in Iraq came to an end, and he returned home safe and sound. The family also provided me and my daughters with shelter when Hurricane Irene swept through New York state just three weeks after Michael died.

I realize that this close relationship to where my family's meat comes from is a privilege, though, and not the norm. I truly hope that changes, for the betterment of our planet and our diets. One hundred percent grass-fed beef is without a doubt more delicious than the conventional meat I grew up eating. A fresh, free-roaming chicken that has spent its days happily pecking along after the cows needs nothing more than a rub of olive oil, sea salt, and freshly ground black pepper. The leftovers transform into tacos (page 109) and chicken patties (page 108)—two of the kids' favorite meals. Meat may play more of a supporting role in our meals now, but the taste takes center stage.

Another option is to buy into a share from a local meat farmer. Flying Pigs Farms in Shushan, New York recently started offering pork shares, which you can divvy up further among friends and family to make it more affordable. This is a good option for beef, too, if it's available in your community.

SICILIAN-STYLE MEATBALLS

As Sinatra said: "Regrets, I have a few"—in my case, a big one is not having spent a day in the kitchen with my Aunt Barbara. An invitation to her house for Sunday gravy—a hearty tomato sauce simmered for hours with meats like pork, beef, and braciola that had been browned in the pot first—was a coveted event. I have many memories of watching her fry up meatballs, but never actually cooked with her before she had a stroke eight years ago.

The seasoning in her meatballs was perfectly balanced with hints of garlic, Locatelli cheese, and fresh parsley. I've kept those flavors prominent, but my meatballs are quite different from hers. For starters, I soak my bread in milk, not water as she did—a measure I imagine was born of thrift since that's how my nana, a single mother of four children in the 1950s, did it. I have a faint memory of also watching my nana fry up meatballs in a tiny galley kitchen, just two blocks from where I now live with her great-grandchildren.

I also use a blend of pork and beef. The real game changer, though, came on the day I tasted the meatballs at Frankies 457, a local Italian restaurant. They were laced with pine nuts and currants. Now, the family recipe I'm handing down to my girls is a mix of memories from my past and present.

MAKES 18 MEATBALLS

Extra-virgin olive oil, for greasing the pan

1/2 cup (125 ml) milk, warmed

2 thick slices white country bread, torn into pieces

1 pound (453 grams) fresh ground beef

1 pound (453 grams) fresh ground pork

1/2 cup (56 grams) freshly grated Locatelli Pecorino Romano cheese

Handful of fresh flat-leaf parsley, finely chopped

2 garlic cloves, minced

2 large eggs, separated

1/2 cup (58 grams) dried currants

1/4 cup (38 grams) pine nuts

1/4 teaspoon freshly ground black pepper

1/2 teaspoon (3 grams) fine sea salt

Preheat the oven to 400° (200°C). Grease a rimmed 11-inch x 17-inch (27-cm x 43-cm) baking sheet with olive oil.

Place the milk in a small bowl and add the bread. Submerge it completely and let it soak for 10 minutes. Squeeze the bread until it's moist but no longer soggy. Discard the remaining milk. Combine the bread with the beef, pork, cheese, parsley, garlic, egg yolks, currants, pine nuts, and salt and pepper in a deep bowl. Use your hands to mix well until everything is combined—you can use a spoon or spatula for this step, but using your hands really helps work the flavors into the ground meat.

Shape the mixture into 18 equal-sized balls. Add the egg whites to a shallow bowl and beat them lightly. Dab your fingertips into the egg whites and gently rub the meatballs to coat them. Place the meatballs on the prepared pan 2 inches (5 cm) apart. Bake for 25 minutes, turning the meatballs halfway through, until they're nicely browned and cooked through. Serve hot or add to a pot of marinara sauce (page 27) and let them simmer until ready to serve.

MAKE AHEAD You can prep the meatball mixture up to four hours in advance. Just cover and store it in the fridge until you're ready to shape and cook them.

FREEZE IT! Place the cooked meatballs in a plastic zip-top bag and store them in the freezer for up to two months. To heat, add them to a pot of marinara sauce (page 27), bring to a boil, and cook until they're heated through, 20 to 25 minutes. The cooking time and amount of sauce you need depends on how many meatballs you're heating— aim for at least 1/2 cup of sauce per meatball.

EASY GLUTEN-FREE Swap in your favorite gluten-free bread and everyone can enjoy these meatballs.

BEEF SPEZZATINO

Stew is one of my favorite meals on a blustery day. What I love most about this recipe is that there's no need to brown the meat beforehand, which means less mess and easier cleanup. A loaf of crusty bread is a must for sopping up the sauce.

MAKES 4 TO 6 SERVINGS

1 (28-ounce/793-gram) can whole peeled San Marzano tomatoes

2 pounds (896 grams) beef stew meat, cut into 1-inch (2.5-cm) chunks

5 medium carrots, peeled and cut into 1-inch (2.5 cm) pieces

2 garlic cloves, chopped

2 tablespoons (28 grams) unsalted butter, cut into 8 pieces

¼ cup (62 ml) extra-virgin olive oil

1 bay leaf

½ cup (125 ml) dry red wine

⅛ teaspoon ground cloves

Sea salt and freshly ground black pepper

1 large Yukon gold potato, peeled and cubed

104

HOMEMADE
with
Love

Add the tomatoes and their juices to a deep bowl and squeeze between your hands to crush them. Set aside.

Place the beef and carrots in a heavy-bottomed, deep skillet. Sprinkle the garlic and pieces of butter over the meat and carrots. Drizzle the olive oil on top. Add the bay leaf and turn the flame onto medium-high heat and cook, without stirring, for 15 minutes.

Stir in the wine. Raise the heat to high and bring to a vigorous boil for 15 minutes. Stir in the cloves and tomatoes. Cover the skillet, reduce the flame to a simmer, and cook for 1 hour.

Give the stew a stir, and season with salt and pepper to taste. Add the potatoes, cover the skillet again, and continue to simmer for 1 more hour, until the meat is extremely tender, almost falling apart when pierced with a fork.

Remove the bay leaf and toss it. Ladle the stew into deep bowls and serve.

SERIOUSLY DELICIOUS RIBS

For those of us living in cramped city quarters, this recipe is a rib-lovers gift, delivering that smoky, falling-off-the-bone flavor from a home oven by simply adapting the "low and slow" tenets of authentic barbecue. I love making these ribs for large parties since most of the work is hands-off, leaving time to prep other dishes. They shared the spotlight with my crispy buttermilk fried chicken at Mikey's 50th birthday party.

MAKES 4 TO 6 SERVINGS

DRY-RUBBED RIBS

1/2 cup (79 grams) packed dark brown sugar

2 teaspoons (6 grams) sweet paprika

1 teaspoon (3 grams) garlic powder

1/2 teaspoon freshly ground black pepper

1 tablespoon (10 grams) coarse salt

1 teaspoon (2 grams) instant
espresso powder

1/4 teaspoon allspice

1 teaspoon (3 grams) chipotle powder

2 whole slabs pork baby back ribs
(3 to 3 1/2 pounds/1.25 to 1.5 kg total)

BRAISING LIQUID

1 cup (250 ml) sparkling white wine,
like prosecco

2 tablespoons (30 ml) apple cider vinegar

2 tablespoons (30 ml) Worcestershire sauce

1 tablespoon (21 grams) honey

For the dry-rubbed ribs, combine the sugar, paprika, garlic powder, pepper, salt, espresso powder, allspice, and chipotle powder in a bowl. Use a fork to stir until well combined. Rub the mixture evenly all over each rack of ribs, making sure to coat both sides. Place the ribs in separate roasting pans (or in a single layer in one big roasting pan). Cover the pans tightly with heavy-duty foil and place them on the bottom shelf of the fridge, for at least 1 hour or overnight.

When you're ready to cook the ribs, preheat the oven to 250°F (120°C). Combine the wine, vinegar, Worcestershire, and honey in a small pot and bring to a boil over high heat. Remove from the stove, and set aside.

Gently remove the foil from the roasting pans and pour the braising liquid over the ribs. Wrap the pans tightly again with the foil and place them in the oven (side by side, if possible). Cook for 2 1/2 hours, and rotate the pans halfway through if cooking on separate racks.

Remove the ribs from the oven, discard the foil, and pour or spoon the braising liquid into a medium pot. Bring the juices to a boil over high heat, then reduce the heat to low so the mixture bubbles gently. Let it cook until the liquid reduces by half and becomes a thick, syrupy sauce, about 30 minutes.

Preheat the broiler. Brush the glaze on top of each rack of ribs. Place the ribs under the broiler until the glaze begins to caramelize, 1 to 2 minutes (watch carefully, or all your patience will be spoiled by burnt ribs!). Slice between the ribs and serve with the remaining glaze on the side.

A SIMPLE ROAST CHICKEN

The first time I used the roast chicken recipe from Dan at Grazin' Angus Acres, I wasn't prepared for it. He lives in the country with lots of land, and apparently many windows to air out the smoke. I quickly found out that roasting chicken at 500ºF (260ºC) is not ideal for city dwellers, but a minor adjustment to 475ºF (245ºC) cleared up the smoke situation. In addition to cranking up the heat, Dan also taught me that a really good-quality chicken needs nothing more than a rub of olive oil and sprinkling of salt and pepper to be the tastiest and easiest dinner ever.

MAKES 4 SERVINGS

1 (3¹/₂-pound/1.5-kg) whole roasting chicken
Extra-virgin olive oil, for drizzling
Coarse sea salt and freshly ground black pepper

Preheat the oven to 475ºF (245ºC).

Rinse the chicken and pat dry with a paper towel. Place in a roasting pan. Drizzle the top of the chicken with a bit of olive oil. Season generously with salt and pepper, to taste. Roast for 20 minutes, then add ¹/₂ cup (125 ml) of water to the bottom of the pan—this helps prevent the drippings from smoking while making a natural sauce from the juices, called *au jus*. Roast for 40 to 50 minutes more, basting the chicken once or twice, until the juices run clear and an instant-read thermometer inserted in the thigh registers 185ºF (85ºC).

Remove the chicken from the oven and let sit for 5 to 10 minutes before carving.

> **NO TRUSS NECESSARY** Tying up the legs and tucking in the wing tips makes for a pretty-looking chicken, but trussing is totally optional in my book. In fact, I've found that not trussing lets the heat circulate into the center of the chicken, allowing it to cook more quickly.

CUMIN-CILANTRO CHICKEN PATTIES

Tacos are my go-to meal for leftover roasted chicken but one night I decided to mix things up with these patties. It was a risk since the girls can be picky when it comes to textures and spices. It helped to chop the chicken very finely. Another rule of thumb I try to follow when making something new for them is keeping a sense of familiarity. They were already used to fresh cilantro and cumin from taco night, so I decided to stick with them here, too. I used some mini potato rolls to turn the patties into sliders, keeping a few plain for the kids and topping the rest with some Jalapeño Pickled Watermelon Rind (page 224)—a win-win for the whole family.

MAKES 6 (3-INCH/7.5-CM) PATTIES

1^1/2 cups (196 grams) finely chopped roasted chicken (page 107)

^{1}/4 cup (3 grams) fresh cilantro, chopped

1 small yellow onion, finely chopped

^{1}/8 to ^{1}/4 teaspoon ground cumin

1 large egg, lightly beaten

^{1}/4 cup (29 grams) plain breadcrumbs

Canola or grapeseed oil, for frying

Combine the chicken, cilantro, onion, cumin, egg, and breadcrumbs in a medium bowl. Stir well to combine.

Add ^{1}/4 inch (0.75 cm) of oil to a 10-inch (25-cm) skillet. Heat the oil over medium-high heat until shimmering, 1 to 2 minutes. Meanwhile, divide the chicken mixture into 6 equal balls and flatten into ^{1}/2-inch/1.5-cm thick patties. Place the patties in the skillet in batches, so as not to crowd the pan, and cook until golden on the bottom, 2 to 3 minutes. Flip the patties with a spatula and cook for another 2 to 3 minutes until nicely browned on the other side. Transfer the patties to a paper-towel lined dish, and let sit for 1 minute so the excess oil drains off. Serve hot.

FREEZE IT! Let the cooked patties cool completely, then pop them in a plastic zip-top freezer bag and remove as much air as possible. To reheat, place them on a baking sheet and heat in a 350ºF (180ºC) oven for 10 to 15 minutes until heated through.

HOMEMADE *with* Love

TWICE AS NICE TACOS

This is a great way to give new life to leftover roasted chicken, hence the "twice as nice" in the title. Taco night was a ritual for Mikey and me long before we had kids. Back in the day before my cooking prowess became self-evident, tacos were always his domain, and I'd stand to the side and play sous-chef. We reversed roles as years went by, and changed up the look and taste of our taco nights too. Now, I can't imagine using a store-bought salsa when the real thing is so easy to make, and tacos just feel naked without a dollop of guacamole on top. I love setting the fixings out family-style so everyone can dig in and help themselves.

MAKES 4 SERVINGS

8 flour or corn tortillas

2 teaspoons (10 ml) extra-virgin olive oil

1 small onion, finely chopped

1 garlic clove, finely chopped

¼ teaspoon ground cumin

⅛ teaspoon ground cinnamon

Sea salt and freshly ground black pepper

1 tablespoon (21 grams) double-concentrated tomato paste (see page 15)

2 cups (261 grams) shredded roasted chicken (page 107)

Fresh salsa, for serving

Guacamole or fresh sliced avocados, for serving

Shredded Monterey Jack or Cheddar cheese, for serving

Preheat the oven to 350ºF (180ºC). Stack the tortillas in the center of a piece of foil. Wrap the foil around the tortillas to make a packet and place in the oven to warm while you prepare the filling.

Heat the olive oil in a 10-inch (25-cm) skillet over medium heat until it's shimmering, about 1 minute. Add the onion and garlic. Cook until fragrant and lightly golden, 1 to 2 minutes. Add the cumin, cinnamon, salt, and pepper, adjusting seasonings to taste, and stir well. Stir in the tomato paste, scraping up any browned bits of onion from the bottom of the pan. Add the chicken and stir until it's well coated. Stir in ¼ cup to ½ cup of water, just enough to thin the tomato paste into a thick sauce. Reduce the heat to low and let it simmer for 5 minutes, to let the chicken absorb the flavors of the sauce.

Remove the tortillas from the oven and transfer them to a cloth towel-lined basket or dish (a pie plate works nicely for this), and cover them so they stay warm.

Transfer the chicken filling into a deep bowl, and set on the table family-style with the other topping ingredients. Dig in.

DROP BISCUIT CHICKEN POT PIE

This is more than just a recipe for chicken pot pie—it's a meditation on love and loss. Chicken pot pie was Mikey's all-time favorite dish. He used to love the one at River Run, a pub in Tribeca that is now long gone. He'd marvel at the flaky disc of puff pastry topping the crock. It soon became one of my top ten meals to make for him.

As our time together lengthened from days into months, and then years, and my obsession with cooking everything from scratch grew, I swapped in a drop biscuit topping for the puff pastry. No matter what any cook tells you, puff pastry takes time—even the quick versions—and with two kids and a career, that's a scarce ingredient on busy weeknights.

In all my years of recipe development and food writing, this is one I never put to pen and paper—it simply lived in my heart and mind. I was saving it for the day my dream, our dream, of writing my first cookbook came true. The day I set out to officially weigh and record the process was an emotionally charged one. I put on *Bridge Over Troubled Waters*, which was an exercise in musical masochism given my state of mind that day, but it fit the mood I was feeling. Then I puttered around the house and procrastinated because I knew it would take all my strength to do the task at hand. As I peeled the carrots, the first ingredient to prep, "The Only Living Boy in New York" came on. It was Mikey's favorite song, and he'd often listen to it on loop, in deep reflection, strumming his guitar. I reached for my iPod, pressed repeat, and went back to the kitchen while it played on loop for 40 minutes.

As I put the pot pie into the oven, I texted my friend Erin, and explained what I was doing. I knew I couldn't be alone when it was ready to eat. She showed up seconds before the timer went off. I set the cast-iron skillet on the windowsill to snap a shot and then collapsed in her arms crying. As we scooped our servings into bowls, a calm washed over me, and I knew I'd taken one more baby step in a very long, exhausting journey of grief. Making this pot pie was yet another little goodbye to a life I so loved, and to a person who will be a part of my heart and soul forever.

MAKES 4 TO 6 SERVINGS

1 tablespoon (14 grams) unsalted butter

4 medium carrots, peeled and diced

2 tablespoons (18 grams) unbleached all-purpose flour

1 cup (250 ml) chicken stock (page 26)

1/2 cup (125 ml) milk

1 cup (120 grams) cubed leftover roasted chicken (page 107)

1/2 cup (59 grams) frozen peas

Handful of fresh flat-leaf parsley (7 grams), chopped

Fine sea salt and freshly ground black pepper

1/2 batch Fluffy Drop Biscuit dough (page 138), unbaked

(recipe continued on next page)

For the pot pie filling: Melt the butter in an 8-inch (20-cm) cast-iron skillet over medium heat. Add the carrots and cook, 1 to 2 minutes, until they are bright orange and barely tender. Sprinkle the flour over the carrots, and stir vigorously for 1 minute to cook the flour a bit.

Slowly pour in the stock, and then the milk. Raise the heat to medium-high and let it come to a very gentle boil. Immediately reduce the heat to a simmer and let cook for 10 minutes.

Add the chicken, peas, and parsley. Let cook until the carrots are tender, and the peas and chicken are heated through, about 5 more minutes. Season with salt and pepper to taste.

Meanwhile, preheat the oven to 425°F (220°C), and prepare the drop biscuit dough. Drop dollops of the dough over the top of the pot pie filling to mostly cover the surface. Transfer the skillet to the oven and bake for about 18 minutes until the biscuits are golden brown. Serve immediately.

9.

Seafood

OKAY, SO NOT TO GET ON A SOAPBOX OR BE ALL preachy, but there is one very important bit of advice I'd like to give about shopping for fish: Ask where it's coming from before you buy it. There's so much news surrounding the way beef, chicken, and pork are produced in the U.S., but not many people realize how much fish is flown in from other countries, some of which have increasingly polluted waters caused by fish farming. Even sustainable farm-raised fish isn't always a safe bet, since some companies feed their fish animal byproducts. There's also the issue of overfishing and possible extinction of certain species—good heavens, who knew buying a simple fillet required so much thought?

So how do you know the fish you're cooking up is safe for your body and the planet? Do a quick check-in with the Seafood Selector on the Environmental Defense Fund's website (www.edf.org). They categorize varieties as Eco-Best, Eco-OK, and Eco-Worst, with reasons for why the worst ones are not healthy options. Take tuna, for example. Albacore from the U.S. and Canada was noted as an Eco-Best fish as I was writing this book. Imported albacore outside of Canada, though, was on the worst list due to dangerous levels of mercury. Don't be shy about asking questions: you have a right to know. And don't worry, tuna salad lovers—Wild Planet, a line of sustainably caught canned seafood, is readily available at larger grocery stores. Tuna melts were my husband's favorite sandwich, so they hold a special place in my heart.

ORANGE BALSAMIC GLAZED SALMON

Mikey loved salmon, and the crispy skin was his favorite part. The secret to that perfectly cooked skin is a hot nonstick skillet—and patience. Don't fuss with your fish or poke and prod it until the skin is properly browned and crisp. If your kids are finicky when it comes to fish, this might be a good starter meal for them, since the sauce reduces to a sweet citrusy glaze.

MAKES 4 SERVINGS

Freshly squeezed juice of 1 orange

1 teaspoon (7 grams) honey

2 teaspoons (15 ml) balsamic vinegar

4 (3-ounce/84-gram) salmon fillets, preferably center-cut

Sea salt and freshly ground black pepper

Preheat an 8-inch (20-cm) nonstick skillet over medium-high heat.

In a small bowl, whisk together the juice, honey, and balsamic vinegar. Set aside.

Season both sides of each piece of salmon with salt and pepper to taste. Place the fish, skin-side down, in the hot nonstick skillet. Cook until the skin is crispy and well browned, about 2 minutes (be patient and do not move it too soon or the skin will stick). Turn the fish over and cook for 2 more minutes until lightly browned and crisp on the other side. Transfer the fish to a plate.

Add the juice mixture to the skillet. Bring it to a boil and cook until slightly thickened, 1 to 2 minutes. Reduce the sauce to a simmer, with bubbles popping gently to the surface. Return the salmon to the pan. Spoon the sauce over the fish repeatedly, as if bathing it, until the salmon is cooked to your liking— for medium, 1 more minute, and for well-done, 2 to 3 more minutes. Transfer the salmon to a platter and spoon the sauce on top to serve.

EGG-FREE GLUTEN-FREE 30 MINUTES OR LESS DAIRY-FREE

BAKED SOLE
WITH LEMON, OLIVES & HERBS

This is a truly a meal that satisfies but won't weigh you down. Sole is a mild, delicate fish that comes alive with the addition of fresh lemon, briny olives, and a punch of flavor from some fresh oregano or lemon thyme, depending on what you can find at the market. It's also ridiculously easy to prep and practically cooks itself.

MAKES 4 SERVINGS

8 whole lemon sole fillets

Sea salt and freshly ground black pepper

1 lemon, thinly sliced

¼ cup (33 grams) kalamata olives, pitted and cut in half

Handful of fresh oregano or lemon thyme,
    leaves removed and chopped, stems discarded

2 tablespoons (30 ml) extra-virgin olive oil

Preheat the oven to 375ºF (190ºC).

Arrange the fillets in a single layer in a 9-inch x 13-inch (22-cm x 33-cm) roasting pan. Season them with salt and pepper to taste. Scatter the lemon slices on top, and sprinkle the olives and herbs over the fish. Evenly drizzle the olive oil over the fish.

Bake until the sole is opaque in color and flakes easily with a fork, 15 to 18 minutes. Transfer the fish to a platter and spoon the juices over it. Serve immediately.

EGG-FREE GLUTEN-FREE 30 MINUTES OR LESS DAIRY-FREE

A POT OF MUSSELS

I think mussels should be considered a diet food, since removing the
tiny chunks of meat from their shells is such an upper body workout. Okay, so maybe that's
stretching things too far, especially considering we've got wine, butter, and cream in the pot with
the mussels. Still, they are such a fun and satisfying meal, and my kids like them, which was a big
surprise the first time I brought a pot to the table.

As much as I love supporting local fishing industries, I must admit Prince Edward Island (PEI)
mussels are my favorite. They have a sweeter, more consistent flavor, and come already cleaned.
Those tough beards on the outside can make prepping mussels from the farmers' market a time-
intensive process. I know because I've done it!

MAKES 4 SERVINGS

2 tablespoons (30 ml) extra-virgin olive oil

2 garlic cloves, chopped

2 plum tomatoes, seeded and chopped

Freshly ground black pepper

$^1/_4$ cup (62 ml) heavy whipping cream

$^1/_2$ cup (125 ml) white wine

2 tablespoons (14 grams) unsalted butter

1$^1/_2$ pounds Prince Edward Island mussels, rinsed and scrubbed for any remaining beards

Handful of fresh flat-leaf parsley, chopped

119

SEA
FOOD

Heat the oil in a 4$^1/_2$-quart pot over medium heat until it's shimmering. Add the garlic and cook
until it's lightly golden and fragrant, about 1 minute. Add the tomatoes and stir, cooking them for
2 minutes until they collapse a bit. Season with pepper to taste, and stir in the cream and wine. Add
the butter and cook for 2 more minutes.

Add the mussels to the pot and cover it tightly. Cook for 3 to 4 minutes until the mussels pop
open, being careful not to overcook them. Stir the parsley into the pot.

To serve, bring the pot to the table or transfer the mussels and the sauce to a deep serving bowl.
Don't forget a crusty loaf of bread to sop up the sauce, and an empty bowl so everyone has a place to
discard their empty shells.

PAN-SEARED SCALLOPS WITH ORANGE & FENNEL SALAD

Fennel has a strong black licorice-laced flavor that I didn't fully appreciate until a few years ago. Here, it acts as a bed for succulent, sweet scallops. On nights when Mikey came home late, this was the perfect meal to sit down to together—it's quick-cooking and didn't weigh us down late at night, but always made a very satisfying meal. In fact, it has an elegant flair and can easily serve as an appetizer for a special-occasion meal, such as risotto, which tends to be on the heartier, more filling side.

MAKES 4 SERVINGS

½ bulb of fennel, very thinly sliced

1 orange, peeled and cut into wedges

2 tablespoons (30 ml) Basic Vinaigrette (page 231)

12 plump sea scallops

Sea salt and freshly ground black pepper

1 tablespoon (14 grams) unsalted butter

Add the fennel, orange slices, and dressing to a medium bowl. Toss well to combine. Evenly spoon the salad onto four separate plates.

Season the scallops with salt and pepper on each side.

Melt the butter in a nonstick skillet over medium-high heat. Add the scallops to the pan—you may need to do this in batches to avoid overcrowding the pan. Cook until the undersides are nicely browned and the tops are opaque, 2 to 3 minutes. Turn the scallops, and cook on the other side until browned and the scallops are cooked through, 1 to 2 more minutes. Place three scallops on top of the fennel salad in each dish. Serve immediately.

30 MINUTES OR LESS GLUTEN-FREE EGG-FREE

LINGUINE WITH WHITE CLAM SAUCE

Mikey had a few tricks up his sleeve in the kitchen, and they usually
came out of a spiral-bound cookbook he bought before we met, called *365 Ways to Cook Pasta*.
I used to tease him incessantly about that book not being a serious guide to cooking pasta.
Now it's a permanent part of my library as a reminder of our time in the kitchen together.

As he became a more confident cook, he also became comfortable deviating from a recipe and
adding his own touches to it. Together, we tweaked that original clam sauce recipe to make it ours.
The big change was using fresh clams instead of canned ones—the only way to go, in my opinion. I
like a lemony kick, too, so we upped the amount of lemon juice. My final touch was a little bit of butter
in the sauce. It adds much-needed depth to the brothy sauce, helping it cling to the pasta.

MAKES 4 SERVINGS

8 ounces (226 grams) uncooked linguine

2 dozen little neck clams, cleaned, juice reserved, and shells discarded

4 tablespoons (56 grams) unsalted butter

1 tablespoon (15 ml) extra-virgin olive oil

2 garlic cloves, chopped

¹/₈ teaspoon red chili pepper flakes

¹/₂ cup (125 ml) white wine

Freshly squeezed juice of 2 lemons

Freshly ground black pepper

¹/₄ cup (4 grams) fresh flat-leaf parsley (leaves only), chopped

Prepare the pasta al dente according to the package directions, making sure to reserve ¹/₂ cup
(62 ml) of the cooking water before you drain it.

Meanwhile, line a strainer with a piece of cheesecloth and pour the reserved clam juice through it
to remove any shell fragments and sand. Discard any solids left in the cloth. You should have about
1 cup of clam juice remaining. Set it aside until ready to use.

Add the olive oil and butter to a deep skillet over medium heat. Once the butter is melted, add
the garlic and chili flakes. Cook until they're fragrant and the garlic is lightly golden, about 1
minute. Pour in the wine and clam juice, and bring it to a gentle boil. Add the clams and reduce the
flame to a simmer, with just a few bubbles popping to the surface. Cook the clam sauce for 5 minutes. Stir in the lemon juice and season with black pepper to taste.

Add the cooked linguine to the pan and toss well to coat it with the sauce. Cook for 1 to 2 more
minutes to let the pasta absorb some of the sauce. If it seems dry, add some of the reserved pasta
cooking water. Sprinkle the parsley over the pasta and toss well. Divide the pasta among four deep
bowls, and ladle the sauce on top. Serve immediately.

TIME-SAVING TIP I prefer to leave shucking the clams to the pros. Most seafood
markets will do it free of charge; just be sure to ask them to reserve the juice for you.

EGG-FREE · 30 MINUTES OR LESS

WHOLE ROASTED BRANZINO

The first time I served a whole fish for dinner, I fully expected the girls to run from the table. Their reaction was the total opposite, and soon we were all picking over the bones for the last bits of meat. When buying a whole fish, make sure the eyes are nice and clear, as this indicates the fish's freshness. Most fish markets remove the scales, but it's a good idea to run your fingers over the skin just in case they missed a few. Remove them by scraping the flat of your knife against the scales.

MAKES 4 SERVINGS

2 whole branzino, about 1¹/₄ pounds (566 grams) each

Sea salt and freshly ground black pepper

2 tablespoons (28 grams) unsalted butter, cut into 8 pieces

2 garlic cloves, thinly sliced

Handful of fresh flat-leaf parsley

1 lemon, cut into ¹/₈-inch/.25-cm-thick slices

Extra-virgin olive oil, for drizzling

Preheat the oven to 400°F (200°C).

Using a sharp knife, make 3 diagonal slashes into the skin on each side of the fish. Season the inside of both fish with salt and pepper to taste. Stuff each fish with half the garlic, half the parsley, and half the butter. Fit 1 slice of lemon into each cut mark on the skin.

Place the fish into a 9-inch x 13-inch (22-cm x 33-cm) baking dish. Drizzle a little olive oil over each piece, and cook until the meat is white and flakes with a fork, 23 to 25 minutes.

Transfer the fish to a serving platter and spoon any juices that collected in the pan on top. Serve immediately.

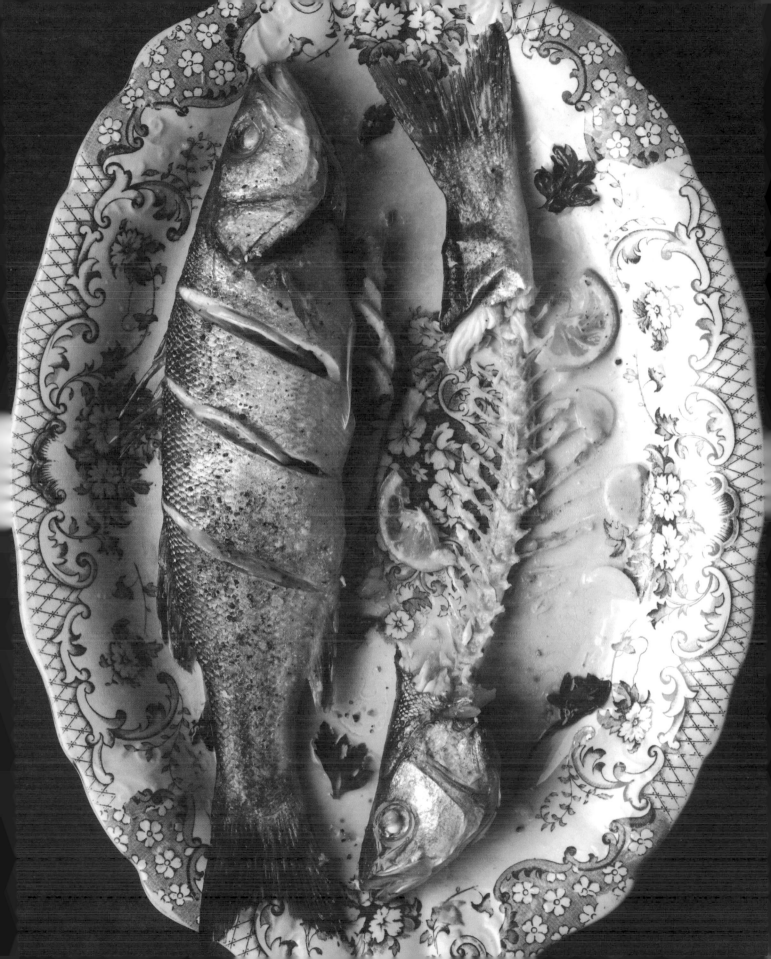

10.

Pizzas, SAVORY TARTS & BREADS

I'VE BEEN MAKING PIZZA FROM SCRATCH FOR almost twenty years now, and have tried a variety of techniques during that time. It would take a whole book to cover the variations. Instead I decided to stick with two of my family's favorites—a classic Neapolitan, basically tomato sauce and fresh mozzarella cheese (or Crispy Thin Crust Pizza, page 128, as I've named it here), and Roasted Vegetable Pizza, page 130. If you want to make pizza like the pros, then using a pizza stone is the way to go. Rest assured, though, that you can still have a mighty tasty pizza without one, so I've included directions for both techniques.

Homemade bread is a treat everyone should try at least once, though chances are your first time won't be your last. Soda breads are a good starter recipe because they don't require proofing time.

I love fruit tarts, but realized my vegetables were getting a bit jealous. The first savory tart I ever made was with summer squash, homemade ricotta and lemon thyme (page 135). It was the perfect summer dinner, paired with a peppery arugula salad, and these tarts have become a regular on my lunch and dinner menus ever since.

HOMEMADE PIZZA DOUGH

After almost twenty years of making pizza, I've learned a thing or two.

First—weather affects your dough: it's that plain and simple. It's almost a Zen practice, and in a way the dough speaks to you, letting you know what it needs. On hot, humid days, the dough drinks up flour, so you'll likely need more during the kneading process. Colder, drier days mean your dough won't be so thirsty, and will need less. This is where visual cues *and* understanding how your dough should feel are so important. The last thing you want is to force-feed more flour than the dough needs. Dough that is ready to start the first rise should be smooth and elastic, and not at all sticky to the touch. You should be able to make an indentation with your finger without any remnants of dough sticking to it.

My second tip is more of a recommendation. Bread flour is your friend when you're making pizza dough. While all-purpose flour works fine, and is an equal gram-for-gram substitution, the higher protein (gluten) content in bread flour gives the dough a boost as it rises and results in a lighter, chewier crust. If you make pizza or bread on a regular basis, then it's well worth the shelf space to keep bread flour on your permanent pantry list.

MAKES TWO (12-INCH/30-CM) THIN CRUSTS
OR ONE (16-INCH/40-CM) THICK CRUST

3 cups (415 grams) unbleached bread flour

1 1/2 teaspoons (6 grams) active dry yeast

1 teaspoon (6 grams) fine sea salt

1 teaspoon (5 grams) granulated natural cane sugar

1 cup (250 ml) warm water (110°F/43°C)

1 tablespoon (15 ml) extra-virgin olive oil

In a deep bowl, whisk together 2 cups of the flour with the yeast, salt, and sugar. Add the water and olive oil. Using a wooden spoon, stir it together to form a wet, sticky dough. Sprinkle 1/2 cup of the remaining flour onto a clean counter or large cutting board. Scrape the dough out onto the board and knead in the flour until the dough is smooth and soft, but not tacky or sticky—you may not need all of it or you may need a little extra (see headnote).

Lightly oil the inside of a deep glass or ceramic bowl. Place the dough in the bowl, cover tightly with plastic wrap, and place in a warm spot until doubled in volume (about 1 1/2 hours).

Once the dough has risen, sprinkle some of the remaining flour, about 2 tablespoons, on your work surface. Turn the dough out and gently knead it once or twice to deflate. If you're making one thick-crust (or deep-dish) pizza, place the dough back in the bowl, cover it tightly with plastic wrap

(recipe continues on next page)

again, and place back in a warm spot until doubled in volume once more (about 30 minutes). For two thin-crust pizzas, lightly oil a second glass bowl. Evenly divide the dough in half, place half in each bowl, cover tightly with plastic wrap, and place both bowls back in a warm spot until doubled in volume once more (about 30 minutes). Proceed as directed to make your pizza.

FREEZE IT! Once the dough has finished its first rise and has been kneaded for a second time, you can wrap it tightly in plastic wrap, toss it in a plastic zip-top bag, and freeze for future use. It will last for up to 2 months in the freezer. The day before you're ready for pizza night, transfer the dough to the fridge so it can thaw. Remove it from the fridge 2 hours before you're ready to make pizza, so it will come to room temperature, rise, and be ready to press out.

HOMEMADE
with
Love

CRISPY THIN CRUST PIZZA

Pizza Friday has been a ritual at our house for about five years now.
I usually get the dough started while the girls are in school, and prep the rest of the ingredients so everything is ready to go when they get home. Virginia pulls her step stool alongside me and loves spreading on the sauce and dropping chunks of fresh mozzarella on top. Isabella clears the coffee table so that once the pies come out of the oven, we can make our way to the sofa and curl up for a pizza and movie night. It's such a peaceful way to say goodbye to the Monday to Friday grind and get ready for a slower weekend pace.

MAKES TWO (12-INCH/30-CM) PIZZAS

1 batch Homemade Pizza Dough (page 127), divided into 2 balls
Extra-virgin olive oil, as needed
1 cup (225 grams) 20-Minute Marinara Sauce (page 27)
8 ounces (226 grams) fresh mozzarella cheese, diced
1 cup (56 grams) freshly grated Pecorino Romano cheese
Freshly ground black pepper

To bake your pizza in the oven without a pizza stone, preheat the oven to 500°F (260°C) with the oven rack adjusted to the center position.

Lightly coat two 12-inch (30-cm) round pizza pans with olive oil. Set one pan aside.

Place one ball of the dough onto the center of one of the pans, and press it out to the edges. Fill a small ramekin or bowl with some olive oil. Lightly brush the outer $\frac{1}{2}$-inch (1.25-cm) border of the dough with oil, using a pastry brush. Spread half of the marinara sauce over the crust, just up until the olive oil border.

Scatter half of the mozzarella across the top. Sprinkle half of the Pecorino Romano cheese on top. Season with pepper to taste and drizzle a very thin swirl of olive oil on top. Bake until the crust is a deep golden color and the cheese is bubbly, about 10 minutes.

Meanwhile, press out the remaining dough on the remaining pan, and prepare it using the same directions, so that the second pie will be ready to bake as soon as the first one comes out of the oven. Cut each pizza into 8 slices and serve hot.

To use a pizza stone in the oven, place a round baking stone on the center rack of your oven. Preheat the oven to 500°F (260°C).

Lightly sprinkle a work surface with flour. Place one ball of dough on the counter and, starting from the center, press it out into a 12-inch (30-cm) circle. Sprinkle a light dusting of flour on a pizza peel or the back of a large baking sheet. Gently fold the dough in half and transfer it to the peel or sheet. Unfold the dough and lay flat.

Fill a small ramekin or bowl with some olive oil. Lightly brush the outer $\frac{1}{2}$-inch (1.25 cm) border of the dough with oil, using a pastry brush. Spread half of the marinara sauce over the crust, just up until the olive oil border. Scatter the mozzarella across the top. Sprinkle the Pecorino Romano cheese on top. Season with pepper to taste and drizzle a very thin swirl of olive oil on top.

Open the oven and, using a quick flick of the wrist (see Pizza Like the Pros, below), slide the pizza off the peel or pan and directly onto the baking stone in the oven. Bake for 8 to 10 minutes until the cheese is bubbling and the crust is golden. Remove the pizza from the stone using the same method, and a flat spatula for help, if needed.

Once the first pizza is cooked, you can go ahead and prepare the second pizza, then cook as directed. Cut each pizza into 8 slices and serve hot.

PIZZA LIKE THE PROS Native New Yorkers, especially those of us hailing from Brooklyn, take our pizza seriously. Cooking a pizza directly on a preheated baking stone at home is as close as you can get to a crust that has all the air pockets and lightness you get at a great pizza parlor. Transferring the pizza onto the stone takes a little practice, but mostly confidence. The important thing to remember as you slide the pizza off the peel and into the oven is to quickly pull your wrist and arm back in a quick jerking motion. It's the exact nudge of force the pizza needs to move in one fell swoop from the peel to the stone.

ROASTED VEGETABLE PIZZA

I love one-dish meals for their ease of clean up, and adding a heaping serving of roasted vegetables to my homemade pizza counts as a perfectly balanced meal. Sometimes I toss a handful of chopped black or kalamata olives in with the veggies, too, depending on my mood. Next to pizza with meatballs, this was Mikey's favorite Friday pizza to come home to.

MAKES ONE (16-INCH/40-CM) THICK-CRUST PIZZA

1 batch Homemade Pizza Dough (page 127)

Extra-virgin olive oil, for brushing the crust

$^{1}/_{2}$ cup (112 grams) 20-Minute Marinara Sauce (page 27)

6 ounces (170 grams) fresh mozzarella cheese, cut into cubes

2 cups (358 grams) Easy Roasted Vegetables (page 142)

Freshly grated Pecorino Romano cheese, to taste

To bake your pizza without a pizza stone, preheat the oven to 450ºF (240ºC). Lightly coat a 16-inch (40-cm) round pizza pan with oil.

Place the dough onto the center of the pan and press it out to the edges. Lightly brush the outer $^{1}/_{2}$-inch (1.25-cm) border of the dough with oil, using a pastry brush. Spread the marinara sauce over the crust, just up until the olive oil border. Scatter the mozzarella and vegetables across the top, and then finish with a sprinkling of the Pecorino Romano cheese.

Bake for 20 minutes until the cheese is bubbling and the crust is golden. Remove from the oven and let sit for 1 minute before cutting into 8 slices.

To use a pizza stone, place a pizza baking stone on the center rack of your oven. Preheat the oven to 500ºF (260ºC).

Lightly sprinkle a work surface with flour. Place your dough on the counter and, starting from the center, press it out into a 16-inch (40-cm) circle. Sprinkle a light dusting of flour on a pizza peel or the back of a large baking sheet. Gently fold the dough in half and transfer it to the peel or sheet. Unfold the dough and lay flat.

Lightly brush the outer $^{1}/_{2}$-inch (1.25-cm) border of the dough with oil, using a pastry brush. Spread the marinara sauce over the crust, just up until the olive oil-brushed border. Scatter the mozzarella and vegetables on top, and then finish with a sprinkling of Pecorino Romano cheese.

Open the oven and, using a quick flick of the wrist (see sidebar on page 129), slide the pizza off the peel or pan and directly onto the baking stone in the oven. Bake for 15 to 18 minutes until the cheese is bubbling and the crust is golden. Remove the pizza from the stone using the same method, and a flat spatula for help, if needed. Let the pizza sit for 1 minute before cutting into 8 slices.

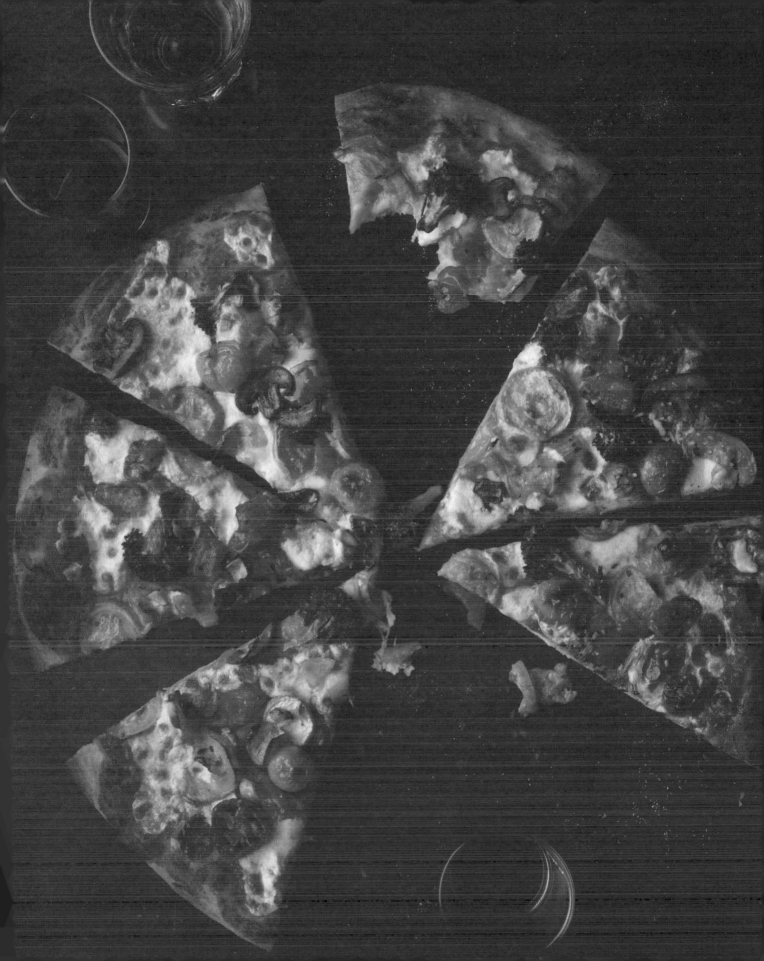

RICOTTA, KALAMATA OLIVE & ARUGULA FOCCACIA

When the weather gets warmer, I crave a lighter spin on my homemade pizza, and this fits the bill. I love the contrast of flavors in this focaccia and the way they complement each other. The olives add a briny, salty quality, the arugula brings a peppery punch, and the creaminess of the fresh ricotta mellows and tames them both.

MAKES 4 TO 6 SERVINGS

1 tablespoon (15 ml) extra-virgin olive oil, plus more for brushing and drizzling

1 batch Homemade Pizza Dough (page 127)

$^1/_2$ cup (113 grams) Creamy Homemade Ricotta (page 32)

$^1/_2$ cup (66 grams) pitted Kalamata olives, minced

Sea salt flakes (I use Maldon) and freshly ground black pepper

1 packed cup (40 grams) arugula

1 tablespoon (5 grams) freshly grated Parmesan cheese

Preheat the oven to 500ºF (260ºC).

Lightly brush a 9-inch x 13-inch (22-cm x 33-cm) rimmed baking sheet with oil. Gently press the dough to the edges of the pan. Drizzle the tablespoon of olive oil over the dough. Drop small dollops of ricotta cheese all over the dough. Sprinkle the olives on top. Season with salt and pepper to taste.

Bake for 10 minutes. Remove the pan from the oven, and scatter the arugula on the top. Drizzle with some olive oil, sprinkle with the Parmesan cheese, and season with more salt, if desired. May be served hot, warm, or even at room temperature.

PIADINI

It wasn't until a few years ago that I discovered Italy has its own version of a pocket-less pita, known as a piadina (its singular spelling). Piadini are quicker to make than pita, though, because they are made with baking powder, not yeast, and don't require any proofing time. They also cook on the stove top in a cast-iron skillet, making them an easy option if you're craving homemade bread for sandwiches. The whole batch comes together in about 30 minutes from start to finish. You can use them as-is for cold sandwiches, but they also make killer panini.

I've taken some liberties with the traditional recipe, first by swapping in olive oil for the lard. Italian nonnas might also take issue that I've left out the milk—the end result is a little lighter than the usual mix of milk *and* water.

MAKES 8 PIADINI

2 cups (294 grams) unbleached all-purpose flour

1¹/₂ teaspoons (5 grams) baking powder

³/₄ teaspoon (3 grams) fine sea salt

2 tablespoons (30 ml) extra-virgin olive oil

Sandwich fillings of your choice

In a medium bowl, whisk together the flour, baking powder, and salt to combine. Using a fork, stir in the olive oil. Pour in ³/₄ cup (187 ml) water and stir with a wooden spoon until the mixture forms a rough dough. Turn out onto a clean work surface (you do not need to flour it beforehand). Knead the dough a few times until it becomes smooth.

Heat a cast-iron skillet over medium-high heat.

Divide the dough into 8 equal pieces. Take a ball of dough and, starting at the center, gently press it out into a circle using your fingertips. Switch to a rolling pin and gently finish rolling it out into an 8-inch (2.5-cm) round. Pierce the surface a few times with the tines of a fork. Repeat with the remaining balls of dough.

Place a piadina in the preheated skillet, and let it cook until golden with some dark or charred spots on the underside (it may also puff up a little), about 2 minutes. Flip the piadina and cook until the other side is golden with a few dark spots as well, 1 to 2 more minutes. Serve warm with the sandwich fillings of your choice.

> **PORTION SIZE** In an effort to control portion sizes, I made these piadini smaller than traditional ones. If you'd like a larger, more authentic size, then divide the dough into 6 pieces instead of 8, and follow the directions from there, rolling them out into 10-inch (25-cm) circles. Just make sure your skillet is large enough that they can lie flat in it.

SUMMER SQUASH, RICOTTA & LEMON THYME TART

I discovered lemon thyme at the farmers' market a few years ago when I was buying herbs to plant in the yard, and have been borderline obsessed with it ever since. It has a citrusy scent, as you might expect, but also a more delicate taste than regular English thyme. In this tart, it adds a faint floral flavor that helps balance out the underlying bitterness of yellow summer squash.

MAKES 6 TO 8 SERVINGS

WHOLE WHEAT PASTRY CRUST

1¹/₂ cups (210 grams) whole wheat pastry flour, plus more for sprinkling

³/₄ teaspoon (4 grams) fine sea salt

¹/₄ teaspoons (1 gram) baking powder

1 teaspoon (4 grams) granulated natural cane sugar

1 stick (112 grams) cold unsalted butter, cut into 16 pieces

3 tablespoons (45 ml) ice cold water

TART FILLING

5 ounces (140 grams) Creamy Homemade Ricotta (page 32)

Freshly grated zest of 1 lemon

1 large summer squash, sliced into ¹/₈-inch (0.31-cm) coins

Extra-virgin olive oil, as needed

4 sprigs fresh lemon thyme

Pinch of smoked paprika

3 tablespoons (6 grams) grated Pecorino Romano cheese

Preheat the oven to 425°F (220°C).

To make the whole wheat pastry crust: Add the flour, salt, baking powder, and sugar to a deep bowl and whisk to combine. Scatter the butter over the dry ingredients and rub together quickly with your fingertips until it forms a sandy-looking texture with some pebble-sized pieces. Sprinkle the cold water over the mixture and stir with a fork until the dough forms a rough ball. Press the dough into a 10-inch (25-cm) tart pan with a removable bottom.

For the tart filling: Stir the ricotta and lemon zest together in a small bowl. Spread the mixture into a thin layer on top of the dough. Arrange the squash slices on top of the ricotta in a circular pattern, overlapping the edges a bit. Drizzle a little olive oil over the squash.

Strip the leaves off the stems of lemon thyme (imagine the motion of a firefighter sliding down a pole). Sprinkle the leaves over the squash, along with the paprika. Scatter the cheese on top of the tart and bake for 20 minutes until the edges and top are golden.

V · EGG-FREE · UNDER 1 HOUR

FRENCH ONION CHEESE BUNS

People often ask how I create new recipes. I wake up thinking about food, and it stays on my mind all day long as I pass shops and farmers' markets. New ideas always seem to be infiltrating my subconscious. One day, while making cinnamon buns, I wondered what it would be like to create a savory version. I decided to infuse the flavor of a French onion soup (page 74) between the folds and rolls of dough. It's a great savory option for breakfast, but also pairs nicely with a salad for a substantial dinner.

MAKES 8 BUNS

Extra-virgin olive oil, for brushing the pan and the dough

1 large egg, lightly beaten

1¹/₂ cups (315 grams) Molasses-Simmered Onions (page 154)

1 batch Homemade Pizza Dough (page 127)

2 cups (125 grams) grated Swiss cheese

Preheat the oven to 350°F (180°C).

Lightly coat a 9-inch (22-cm) deep dish pie pan with olive oil. Add the egg and onions to a small bowl, and stir to mix well.

On a lightly floured board or counter, press the dough out into a 10-inch x 12-inch (25-cm x 30-cm) rectangle. Spread the egg and onion mixture over the dough, leaving a 1-inch (2.5 cm) border. Evenly sprinkle the cheese on top. Roll the dough up lengthwise, on the long edge, and pinch the end seams closed.

Cut the rolled dough into 8 equal pieces. Arrange the pieces, cut-side down, in the prepared pie plate. Once all the pieces are in the pan, press them down gently so they touch. Brush the tops lightly with a bit of olive oil.

Bake until the buns are golden and the cheese is bubbly, 40 to 45 minutes. Remove the pie plate from the oven and set it on a wire rack to cool for 10 minutes before serving.

PISTACHIO SODA BREAD

I started baking soda breads a few years ago. Unlike breads that require yeast, these breads don't need time to rise, so you can enjoy homemade bread in less than an hour. I've made oat, semolina, and now this pistachio variation, which is in honor of Mikey, since pistachios were his favorite nut. I guess cooking *with* them is a way to feel like I'm still cooking for him.

MAKES ONE (8-INCH/20-CM) ROUND LOAF

³/4 cup (84 grams) Homemade Oat Flour (page 22)

2 cups (280 grams) unbleached all-purpose flour, plus more for dusting and sprinkling

³/4 cup (105 grams) shelled raw unsalted pistachios, very finely chopped

2 tablespoons (30 grams) granulated natural cane sugar

2 teaspoons (12 grams) baking soda

1 teaspoon (6 grams) fine sea salt

1^{1}/2 cups (375 ml) plus 2 tablespoons (30 ml) buttermilk

Preheat the oven to 400ºF (200ºC) with the rack adjusted to the center position.

Add the flours, pistachios, sugar, baking soda, and salt to a deep bowl. Whisk together to mix well. Pour in 1^{1}/2 cups (375 ml) of buttermilk and stir with a wooden spoon until just combined.

Lightly a clean work surface with all-purpose flour. Dump the dough onto the surface and knead it briefly, 30 to 60 seconds, until it forms a relatively smooth ball. Place the dough on a lightly floured rimmed baking sheet. Slightly flatten the ball of dough into a 6-inch/15 cm-wide disc.

Brush the sides and top with the remaining buttermilk. Sprinkle the top with 1 to 2 tablespoons (9 to 18 grams) of flour. Using a very sharp knife, slash a deep "X" on the top of the loaf, making sure not to cut all the way through. This ensures a crispier top and helps the bread bake faster.

Bake for 20 minutes, then move the tray to the upper middle rack of the oven and bake for 8 to 10 more minutes until it becomes a deep golden color. It should sound hollow when tapped with your knuckle. Transfer the bread to a wire rack, and let it cool for at least 1 hour before slicing. Any leftover bread will keep for 2 to 3 days, wrapped tightly in parchment paper.

PATIENCE IS A VIRTUE The temptation of hot, freshly baked bread is irresistible, but all your hard work will be wasted if you cut into it too soon. The bread needs time to rest and let the heat dissipate—the bread is still cooking from that residual heat. Cutting into it too soon will result in a sticky, gummy slice, so be sure to wait the full hour.

FLUFFY DROP BISCUITS

I often joke that I'm a Southern belle stuck in the body of an Italian gal from Brooklyn. Ever since I was a kid, I had a curiosity for *real* biscuits—and I'm not talking about the ones that came out of a tube in the refrigerated section. It wasn't until my mid-twenties that I fulfilled my obsession by making them from scratch.

Making proper cutout biscuits isn't difficult, but the dough requires as little touching as possible: pretty much impossible if you're baking with kids. That's why I love drop biscuits. The kids aren't temped to overwork the dough, but they still get to mix the ingredients together and help drop the biscuits on the tray. It took a few rounds before Virginia learned that her lesson that unlike cake batter, there is nothing tasty about raw biscuit dough. Once baked, though, these biscuits are crisp on the outside and airy on the inside. They're especially good slathered with butter and jam.

MAKES ONE DOZEN

2 cups (290 grams) unbleached all-purpose flour

1 tablespoon (15 grams) baking powder

1/4 teaspoon (1 gram) baking soda

1/2 teaspoon (3 grams) fine sea salt

2 teaspoons (14 grams) granulated natural cane sugar

6 tablespoons (84 grams) cold unsalted butter, cut into 12 pieces

1 1/4 cups (312 ml) buttermilk

Preheat the oven to 425ºF (220ºC) with the rack adjusted to the upper middle position.

Add the flour, baking powder, baking soda, salt, and sugar to a deep bowl. Whisk to combine. Scatter the butter over the dry ingredients and rub together quickly with your fingertips, until it forms a sandy-looking texture with some pebble-sized pieces. Pour in the buttermilk and stir until it just comes together into a thick dough and there are no visible signs of flour. This step should only take a minute: be careful not to overmix the dough.

Drop by scant 1/4-cupfuls onto an ungreased baking sheet—I use an ice cream scoop for this so they come out even in size and shape. Bake until golden on the bottoms and around the edges, 15 to 17 minutes. Serve hot.

Variation: Parmesan & Black Pepper Biscuits

Add 1/2 cup (39 grams) grated Parmesan cheese and 1/4 teaspoon freshly ground black pepper to the dry ingredients and whisk to combine. Proceed with rubbing in the butter and stirring in the buttermilk. After dropping 1/4-cupfuls onto the baking sheet, brush the tops with 1 tablespoon (14 grams) of melted unsalted butter before baking.

11.

Sides
&VEGETABLES

M Y EARLY MEMORIES OF BRUSSELS SPROUTS are from daycare days. They were a murky green color—much like that popular shade of many 1970s appliances—and they smelled quite awful. The experience was enough to turn me off of them for decades. Then I started working at Gramercy Tavern and discovered that Brussels sprouts could be delicious in ways I'd never imagined. The key, as with any variety of cabbage, is not to overcook them—that's what causes the funky aroma. Needless to say, I've expanded my love for all vegetables way beyond the usual side suspects of canned green beans and corn that we ate growing up.

EASY ROASTED VEGETABLES

I love the options that abound from a simple pan of roasted vegetables.
You can serve them as a side to roast chicken or grilled steak, but they're also a hearty vegetarian main course when served over rice or pasta. My other favorite use for them is as a pizza topping (page 130).

SERVES 6

1 yellow summer squash, sliced into coins

1 red bell pepper, diced

$^1/_2$ pint (140 grams) cherry tomatoes, stems removed

6 white button or baby bella mushrooms, sliced

1 small head of broccoli, florets only save stalks for later (page 160)

1 small onion, diced

1 to 2 tablespoons (15 ml to 30 ml) of extra-virgin olive oil

Fine sea salt and freshly ground black pepper, to taste

Preheat the oven to 400ºF.

Add all of the ingredients to a 10-inch (25-cm) cast iron skillet or 9-inch x 13-inch (22-cm x 33-cm) roasting pan. Toss well to coat. Bake for 25 minutes, stirring halfway through, until the broccoli is tender.

Use immediately or let cool completely and store in a covered container in the fridge for up to three days.

HOMEMADE *with* Love

MAKE AHEAD   GLUTEN-FREE   VEGAN   UNDER 1 HOUR

GINGER-LIME SLOW-ROASTED CARROTS

My daughters are quite decisive about their veggies, which is really just another way of saying "picky." Carrots are one of their favorites, though, so I try to mix things up and think outside the "steamed with butter" box. Rainbow carrots, if you can find them, make this simple side look especially pretty, and are a hit with little girls. There are enough interesting flavors happening here to grab my attention, like ginger and lime, and the maple syrup brings out the natural sweetness of the carrots to keep the kids happy.

MAKES 4 SERVINGS

1 (1½-inch/3.75-cm) piece fresh ginger, peeled and finely chopped

1 tablespoon (15 ml) pure maple syrup

1 tablespoon (15 ml) extra-virgin olive oil

Freshly grated zest of 1 lime

Sea salt

1 bunch (450 grams) carrots, peeled and stems discarded

Preheat the oven to 300ºF (150ºC).

Add the ginger, syrup, oil, lime zest, and salt to a small bowl. Adjust seasonings to taste. Beat with a fork to mix well.

Arrange the carrots in a 9-inch x 13-inch (22-cm x 33-cm) roasting pan. Pour the ginger-oil mixture over them, tossing the carrots to coat them well. Bake until tender when pierced with a fork, about 1 hour and 15 minutes. They taste great served hot, room temperature, or even cold.

SIZE MATTERS Thin carrots are best for this dish, since they cook more quickly and look pretty on the plate when presented whole. No worries, though, if all you can get are thicker ones. Just cut them into ½-inch thick coins before roasting.

VEGAN GLUTEN-FREE

SAUTÉED BEET GREENS

I often joke about wanting to write a "waste-free cookbook," but as you can imagine that title wouldn't exactly fly off the shelves. I do have one simple wish, though, and that is for people to see the potential in every part of an ingredient. In the same way "nose to tail" has become a cooking trend with chefs, a similar approach can be taken with vegetables.

Take beets, for example. How many times have you discarded the leafy greens on top? Next time you buy a bunch, save those parts— it's a great way to get more bang for your buck! The leaves can be quite bitter, so I like to tame them with two tricks—sautéed onions, which add a natural sweetness, and blood oranges, which add an aromatic citrus flavor.

MAKES 2 SERVINGS

2 tablespoons (28 grams) unsalted butter

1 small onion, thinly sliced

1 bunch (200 grams) beet greens, rinsed and patted dry, with center ribs removed

1 blood orange, cut into $1/8$-inch/0.31 cm-thick slices (leave the rind on)

Melt the butter in a 10-inch (25-cm) skillet over medium-low heat. Add the onions and cook until they're golden and slightly softened, about 10 minutes.

Meanwhile, roughly chop the beet greens. Add them to the pan, along with the oranges. Stir to mix well. Add $1/2$ cup (125 ml) of water, and cover the skillet. Cook until the greens are wilted and tender, 5 to 7 minutes. Stir once more before serving.

SIMPLE SUBSTITUTION Blood oranges are usually only available in the early winter months here in the Northeast. Once they go out of season, I switch to regular oranges for this recipe.

SWEET POTATO, LEEK & RICOTTA SOUFFLÉ

I originally created this recipe for our Passover dinner a few years ago.
It was around the same time that Virginia was starting to eat solid foods, and I was inspired by all the sweet potatoes I'd been mashing for her meals. I used the food processor here to ensure a super smooth soufflé, but if you're less fussy, you can totally hand-mash your sweet potatoes with a fork.

MAKES 6 SERVINGS

3 tablespoons (84 grams) unsalted butter, at room temperature, divided

1 leek, thinly sliced

4 eggs, separated

2 large sweet potatoes, roasted, peeled, and flesh scooped out and puréed

1 cup (200 grams) Creamy Homemade Ricotta, well-drained (page 32)

Sea salt and freshly ground black pepper

Preheat the oven to 350°F (180°C). Grease the bottom and sides of a 9-inch (22-cm) ceramic or glass pie plate with 1 tablespoon (14 grams) of the butter.

Heat another tablespoon of the butter in a skillet over medium-low heat. Add the leeks and cook them until tender and fragrant, about 5 minutes, stirring occasionally. Remove the pan from the heat when done, and set aside until ready to use.

Meanwhile, using the whisk attachment on your stand or hand mixer, beat the egg whites until stiff peaks form. Set aside.

In a separate medium-sized bowl, mix together the sweet potato purée, remaining tablespoon of butter, ricotta, egg yolks, and salt and pepper together to taste. Stir in the leeks. Gently fold in the egg whites. Spoon the filling into the prepared pie plate and bake for 1 hour until it's puffed and golden. Serve immediately.

REFRIED LENTILS

Taco night is always a hit in my house (page 109). One day, in a rush to get dinner ready, I discovered I was all out of pinto beans. I did find some cooked lentils in the fridge, however, and decided to swap them into my regular refried beans recipe. Sometimes running out of an ingredient is the best inspiration for shedding new light on an old favorite.

MAKES 2 TO 4 SERVINGS

2 slices thick-cut bacon, chopped

1 small onion, finely chopped

1 garlic clove, finely chopped

1¹/₂ cups (425 grams) cooked lentils, puréed

Fine sea salt and freshly ground black pepper

Heat a skillet over a medium flame. Add the bacon and cook until it becomes browned and crispy, 3 to 4 minutes. Use a slotted spoon to transfer it to a plate.

Add the onion and garlic to the skillet and cook until they're golden, 1 to 2 minutes (you can add a little olive oil if the onion and garlic start to stick to the pan).

Add the lentils to the skillet, along with the cooked bacon. Add salt and pepper to taste. Stir well to mix everything together. Reduce the heat to medium-low, and cook until the lentils are heated through, about 5 minutes. Remove the skillet from the heat and cover, or transfer to a covered casserole dish to keep warm until ready to serve.

SAUTÉED SPINACH WITH SHALLOTS & DRIED CHERRIES

A quick sauté with garlic and oil is my go-to prep for just about any leafy green. Sometimes you have to up your game though, especially when company is coming. That's where this recipe comes in. It's the same premise—heating olive oil and sautéing an aromatic— except this time, shallots stand in for garlic and the dried cherries temper the earthy flavor of the spinach. It's an effortless way to wake up your taste buds. If you, like Virginia, are not a fan of dried cherries, feel free to swap in raisins or dried currants.

MAKES 4 SERVINGS

2 teaspoons extra-virgin olive oil

1 shallot, thinly sliced

¼ cup (45 grams) dried cherries

4 cups (170 grams) packed baby spinach, well rinsed and dried

Sea salt and freshly ground black pepper

Heat the olive oil in a deep nonstick skillet over medium-low heat. Add the shallot and cook until fragrant, about 1 minute. Add the cherries, and cook until the shallot is tender, 2 to 3 more minutes. Add the spinach and cook until it's wilted, about 2 minutes. Season with salt and pepper to taste, and give it a good stir to mix well. Serve hot.

CRISPY SPINACH-RICOTTA LATKES

One summer day, I went on a spinach-buying binge at the farmers' market.
Then I got home and realized I needed to find a way to actually get my daughters to eat it—they'd never been fans before. Latkes were always a hit at Hanukkah, and they seemed like a perfect vehicle for getting the girls to give spinach a try again. It isn't really hidden in here, as you can clearly see the tufts of spinach spilling out the sides, but tucking it into crisp potato pancakes was definitely the way to go.

MAKES 10 TO 12 LATKES

1 large russet potato, peeled

1/2 cup (95 grams) packed, very well-drained steamed spinach, chopped

1/2 cup (100 grams) Creamy Homemade Ricotta, well-drained (page 32)

1 large egg, lightly beaten

2 tablespoons (14 grams) freshly grated Parmesan cheese

Pinch of freshly grated nutmeg

Sea salt and freshly ground black pepper

Canola oil, for frying

Fill a large bowl with ice water. Shred the potato into the bowl of ice water. When done, use a strainer or slotted spoon to transfer the shredded potato onto a kitchen towel—do not discard the water in the bowl. Gently squeeze the towel around the potatoes to absorb any excess water. Let the reserved liquid sit undisturbed in the bowl for 10 minutes so the starch can settle to the bottom.

Meanwhile, mix together the spinach, ricotta, egg, and Parmesan in a deep bowl. Add the nutmeg, and season with the salt and pepper to taste. Carefully pour out the water from the reserved liquid bowl, making sure to save the starch that has collected at the bottom. Spoon the starch into the bowl with the spinach mixture. Add the shredded potatoes and give it a good stir to combine.

Fill a skillet with 1/4 inch (0.75 cm) of canola oil and heat over a medium flame. Drop generous tablespoonfuls of the spinach-potato mixture into the heated oil. Cook until golden, about 4 to 5 minutes, then flip and cook for another 4 to 5 minutes until golden on the other side. Transfer to a parchment or paper towel-lined baking sheet to drain. Sprinkle with a bit of sea salt immediately, if desired. Serve warm.

> **MAKE AHEAD** These also reheat with delicious results in a preheated 350ºF (180ºC) oven for about 6 minutes. Just flip them over halfway through. If you really want to plan ahead, make a double batch and freeze the cooled leftovers in a zip-top plastic bag. I'd also suggest these for brunch parties instead of roasted potatoes or home fries, since they're an easy dish to prep in advance.

OLIVE OIL & FETA MASHED TURNIPS

I have an unabashed love for mashed potatoes, so when I set out to develop recipes for this book and spied a big bunch of turnips at the farmers' market, it was only natural for me to want to make a mash with them. The feta addition was inspired by mashed potatoes I had at Cat Cora's restaurant Kouzzina in Disney World (no kidding!). There's a lot of flavor in just one spoonful, between the feta's sharp, creamy flavor and the pungent earthiness of the turnips.

MAKES 4 TO 6 SERVINGS

3 large turnips, cubed

2 medium Yukon gold potatoes, cubed

1 tablespoon (15 ml) extra-virgin olive oil

3 tablespoons (42 grams) unsalted butter

4 ounces (112 grams) feta cheese

Fine sea salt and freshly ground black pepper

1 teaspoon (1 gram) chopped fresh dill

Add the turnips and potatoes to a 3½-quart pot. Fill it with enough water to cover the vegetables. Bring to a boil over high heat. Reduce the heat to medium-high and cook until the turnips and potatoes are fork-tender, 7 to 9 minutes.

Drain the vegetables and add them back to the pot. Cook over high heat for 1 minute, stirring vigorously, to dry out any remaining water. Remove the pot from the heat. Add the olive oil, butter, and feta cheese. Use a potato masher to crush the vegetables until they're mostly smooth—a few chunks are fine. You can use a fork to get the job done, too.

Season with salt and pepper to taste. Spoon into a serving bowl, sprinkle the dill on top, and serve while hot.

SHEEP VS. GOAT Feta is available in two main varieties. A classic Greek feta, made from goat's milk, is salty and sharp-tasting. Personally, I prefer French feta, made with sheep's milk, for its creamier, milder flavor.

EGG-FREE · V · 30 MINUTES OR LESS · GLUTEN FREE

SLOW-ROASTED TOMATOES

These tomatoes are key for making my Slow-Roasted Tomato and
Fresh Mozzarella Panzanella on page 64, but they're certainly not a one-trick pony. Once tomato season hits, keeping a jar in the fridge allows me to make spur-of-the-moment snacks like bruschetta—simply spread fresh ricotta (page 32) on a toasted baguette and top it with a spoon of these tomatoes. Toss the tomatoes with some hot pasta and you've also got an incredibly easy weeknight meal. After the tomatoes are used up, the remaining oil is great as a stand-in for the extra-virgin olive oil in my Basic Vinaigrette (page 231).

MAKES ABOUT 1½ CUPS (380 GRAMS)

1 pint (280 grams) grape tomatoes, cut in half
¼ cup (62 ml) extra-virgin olive oil
Fine sea salt and freshly ground black pepper
6 sprigs fresh lemon thyme, chopped

Preheat the oven to 250º F (120ºC). Add all the ingredients to an 8-inch (20-cm) square baking dish and toss well to coat. Adjust seasonings to taste. Bake until the tomatoes are slightly collapsed and tender, about 1 hour. Let cool completely, and store in a tightly covered mason jar or container in the fridge for up to 2 weeks.

MOLASSES-SIMMERED ONIONS

If you thought this recipe seemed similar to the base for my French
onion soup (page 74), then give yourself a gold star, Encyclopedia Brown (yes, I've just dated
myself with that reference). One day, as I was making the soup, it occurred to me that the onions
would be delicious tucked into savory rolls (page 136), in a frittata, served on top of burgers, and
in a host of other uses I've yet to discover. They also make for an excellent side dish with grilled
flank steak.

MAKES ABOUT 4 CUPS (840 GRAMS)

4 tablespoons (56 grams) unsalted butter

1 tablespoon (15 ml) extra-virgin olive oil

3 Vidalia onions, thinly sliced

2 teaspoons (12 grams) fine sea salt

Freshly ground black pepper

1 tablespoon (15 ml) molasses

1 teaspoon (5 ml) sherry vinegar

Add the butter and olive oil to a 4½-quart (4-L) stockpot over medium-high heat. Once the butter
has melted, add the onions and season them with the salt, and add pepper to taste. Cover the pot
and let the onions cook until they are slightly tender, stirring occasionally, about 20 minutes.

Remove the lid and stir in the molasses and vinegar, making sure to scrape up any browned bits at
the bottom of the pot. Reduce the heat to low and cook uncovered until the onions are very tender,
and the liquid has reduced by half, 30 to 40 minutes. Let the onions cool completely and store in a
tightly covered container for up to 1 week.

BROWN BUTTER BRUSSELS SPROUTS & BUTTERNUT SQUASH

I can't believe I didn't fall for Brussels sprouts until my late twenties.
Now I eagerly await fall for the start of the season. They make for an excellent raw salad, simply shaved and tossed with my Basic Vinaigrette (page 231). But when I'm feeling indulgent, I like to make this dish. Starting the bacon in a cold pan is the easiest way to ensure the pan doesn't overheat—a big help, since dinnertime is an elaborate juggle of homework, hot pans, and a four-year-old tethered to my leg.

MAKES 4 TO 6 SERVINGS

3 ounces (84 grams) smoked thick-cut bacon, roughly diced

2 tablespoons (28 grams) unsalted butter

2 cups (276 grams) diced butternut squash

1 small shallot, thinly sliced

10 ounces (280 grams) Brussels sprouts, tough ends trimmed, cut in half

Salt and freshly ground black pepper

Add the bacon to a cold skillet and place over medium-high heat. Cook the bacon until it's crispy, stirring occasionally. Using a slotted spoon, transfer the bacon to a paper towel-lined plate.

Add the butter to the skillet and cook until it turns a deep golden color (it will also have a nutty, fragrant scent). Add the butternut squash to the pan and cook for 5 minutes, stirring occasionally, until it's caramelized and lightly browned. Add the shallot and Brussels sprouts and season with salt and pepper to taste. Cook until the Brussels sprouts are just tender, 7 to 10 more minutes. Return the cooked bacon to the skillet, and give it a good stir before serving.

MAKE IT A MEAL Toss the finished dish with some cooked pasta for an easy one-bowl meal. Top with freshly grated Parmesan cheese before serving, if desired.

EGG-FREE   30 MINUTES OR LESS   GLUTEN-FREE

12.
Snacks

YOU KNOW HOW PEOPLE JOKE ABOUT HAVING A SWEET tooth? Well, I'd swear Mikey had a snack tooth, and I'm pretty sure our younger daughter inherited it. In an effort to create some better-for-you snacking habits, I started experimenting with homemade popcorn. If you've never had kernels popped in some olive oil on the stovetop, then you're in for a real treat. Popcorn is a blank canvas of sorts, and on the nights when Mikey and I had time to relax with a movie on the couch, I liked to gussy it up with fresh rosemary and Pecorino Romano cheese (page 166).

I also try to keep some healthier homemade snacks for that danger zone between school and dinnertime. The kids need a little something to tide them over, and it was while cooking dinner one night that I decided to turn some broccoli stalks into a snacktime dip (page 160). And let's not forget the thousands of lunches I've packed since my older daughter, Isabella, started elementary school. One day, I'll calculate exactly how much money I've saved by making my own granola bars (page 159).

ZUCCHINI PARMESAN HUMMUS

Once zucchini starts flooding the farmers' markets, I get a little greedy, and sometimes buy more than I can possibly eat in a few days. In those cases, I throw it on the grill, store the leftovers in the fridge, and dip into my "stash" when I'm looking for inspiration. It just so happened that one day, I also had leftover chickpeas in the fridge. It wasn't enough to make a whole batch of hummus, so I decided to add zucchini to stretch it out.

MAKES ABOUT 2 CUPS (455 GRAMS)

1 cup (280 grams) chickpeas, drained and rinsed

1 medium zucchini, roasted or grilled and cut into chunks

Freshly squeezed juice of 1 lemon

1/4 cup (25 grams) grated Parmesan cheese

Sea salt and freshly ground black pepper

3 tablespoons (35 ml) extra-virgin olive oil, plus more for serving

Add the chickpeas, zucchini, lemon juice, cheese, salt, and pepper to the bowl of a food processor. Process until the mixture forms a chunky paste, about 45 seconds. Slowly drizzle in the oil and continue processing until the hummus becomes smooth and creamy, about 1 minute.

Spoon the hummus into a shallow bowl and top with a swirl of olive oil before serving.

MAKE AHEAD The hummus may be made up to two days in advance. Let it come to room temperature before serving.

15-MINUTE GRANOLA BARS

Isabella and Virginia are like their daddy in that they love nibbling on sweet or salty treats, which is why we have an officially sanctioned snack drawer. While it has been known to house an occasional lollipop, it's mostly filled with things like raisins, nuts, fruit purée pouches, and these granola bars. They're a hit with the neighborhood kids when I pack them in the girls' lunchboxes.

MAKES ONE DOZEN BARS

¹/₄ cup (95 grams) brown rice syrup

1 teaspoon (5 ml) extra-virgin olive oil

2 tablespoons (24 grams) packed light or dark brown sugar

2¹/₂ cups (277 grams) granola (page 23)

Preheat the oven to 350°F (180°C). Line an 8-inch (20-cm) square glass baking dish with parchment paper, letting the paper hang over the sides of the pan.

Combine the brown rice syrup, oil, and sugar in a small, heavy-bottomed pot. Bring to a boil, then reduce to a simmer, and cook until the sugar is completely dissolved, about 2 minutes.

Add the granola to a large heatproof bowl. Pour the syrup mixture over the granola, stirring well with a nonstick rubber spatula. Scrape the mixture into the prepared baking dish, and spread it out into an even layer.

Bake for 15 minutes until slightly golden. Remove from the oven and let it cool completely on a wire rack. Cut into 12 equal-sized bars. Store in an airtight container for up to 1 week, though they'll likely disappear in a few days' time.

READ YOUR LABELS I prefer to use homemade granola for these bars, but you can certainly use a store-bought one instead. Be sure to read the labels. Just because it's granola doesn't mean it's filled with healthy ingredients—many brands actually contain high-fructose corn syrup or partially hydrogenated oils.

30 MINUTES OR LESS · GLUTEN-FREE · VEGAN

ROASTED BROCCOLI DIP

Let's face it: broccoli stems are a tough sell. They're just not as pretty as the florets, which is why supermarkets charge a premium for just the crowns (basically the florets with the stems cut off). Why should you pay more and get less? Buy the whole bunch, trim it yourself, and make this dip with the leftover stalks.

This dip is more like a tapenade than a dip, making it perfect to spread on toasted baguette. But dip just has a more kid-friendly ring to it, and getting them to happily eat their broccoli is another goal of this recipe. Bonus: it doubles as a pesto-like sauce when tossed with hot pasta.

MAKES 1¼ CUPS (271 GRAMS)

3 cups coarsely chopped broccoli stems
  (from about 1 medium head of broccoli)

1 garlic clove, crushed

2 teaspoons (10 ml) extra-virgin olive oil

Sea salt and freshly ground black pepper

Freshly squeezed juice of ½ lemon

2 teaspoons (5 grams) grated Parmesan cheese

½ cup (112 grams) plain Greek yogurt

⅛ teaspoon ground cinnamon

Carrot sticks, for serving

Parmesan Black Pepper Pita Chips, for serving (page 168)

Preheat the oven to 400°F (200°C).

Toss the broccoli, garlic, and olive oil together in an 8-inch (20-cm) square baking dish. Season with salt and pepper to taste. Bake until the stem pieces are tender when pierced with a fork, 18 to 20 minutes.

Scrape the broccoli mixture into the bowl of a food processor. Add the lemon juice, cheese, and half of the yogurt. Pulse 2 to 3 times to break the broccoli up a bit, then process 1 to 2 minutes until it becomes a chunky pesto-like consistency. Transfer to a bowl, stir in the remaining yogurt and the cinnamon, adjusting the flavor with salt and pepper, if necessary. Serve with carrot sticks and pita crisps.

EGG-FREE · V · 30 MINUTES OR LESS · GLUTEN-FREE

CREAMY ONION DIP

My aunt used to make a killer onion dip when I was a kid, and it wasn't until years later that I learned it came from the back of a dried soup mix box (yes, that one). This is my homemade version based on the same flavors but without all the fillers and artificial ingredients. I gave it a healthier makeover by swapping in some Greek yogurt for the sour cream normally used. It adds a nice tang that balances the sweetness of the caramelized onions.

MAKES ABOUT 1 CUP (198 GRAMS)

2 teaspoons (10 ml) extra-virgin olive oil
1 medium yellow onion, thinly sliced
Salt and freshly ground black pepper
$1/3$ cup (80 grams) sour cream
$1/3$ cup (75 grams) Greek yogurt

Heat the olive oil in a skillet over medium heat. Add the onion and season to taste with the salt and pepper. Cook until the onion begins to soften and becomes golden, about 8 minutes, stirring occasionally. Cover the skillet and reduce the heat to medium-low. Cook until the onion is very tender, about 10 more minutes. Transfer the onion to a bowl, scraping up any browned bits at the bottom of the pot, and let it cool for at least 10 minutes (this step may be done up to 1 day in advance).

Add the onion, sour cream, and yogurt to the bowl of a food processor and pulse until well mixed and the onion is mostly, but not completely, chopped. Alternatively, if you don't have a food processor, you can chop the onion very finely by hand and fold all the ingredients together with a rubber spatula. The dip may be stored in an airtight container in the fridge for up to 2 days.

EGG-FREE MAKE AHEAD V 30 MINUTES OR LESS

HOMEMADE CHEESE CRACKERS

My girls love a certain cheesy cracker shaped like a fish, but I'm not so crazy about the ingredients. As usual, I took matters into my own hands and set out to make a homemade version to evoke memories of my own childhood—my beloved Cheez-Its.

After years of making these crackers, and just cutting the butter into pieces, I decided to try shredding it instead, since the grater was already out from preparing the cheese. I found it helped disperse the butter better in the dough, and I've been doing it that way ever since. I went for a milder flavored cracker (kid-talk for not spicy), but you can certainly add some punch with a hit of cayenne or chipotle, or by doubling the amount of mustard powder.

MAKES 11 TO 12 DOZEN

1 1/2 cups (216 grams) whole wheat pastry flour, plus more for sprinkling

1/2 teaspoon (3 grams) fine sea salt

1/4 teaspoon (1 gram) sweet paprika

1/4 teaspoon (1 gram) dry mustard powder

2 cups (170 grams) shredded Cheddar cheese

1 stick (112 grams) very cold unsalted butter, shredded using a box grater

2 tablespoons (15 ml) cold seltzer

Preheat the oven to 400° (200°C). Line two 9-inch x 13-inch (22-cm x 33-cm) baking sheets with parchment paper.

Add the flour, salt, paprika, and mustard powder to the bowl of a food processor. Pulse once or twice to blend. Add the cheese and butter. Pulse until the mixture forms a sandy texture. Pour in the seltzer and pulse a few more times, just until a ball of dough forms.

Divide the dough into two equal pieces. Place half between two sheets of parchment paper and set the other half aside. Roll out to an 1/8-inch (0.31-cm) thickness. Lift one side of the parchment, and sprinkle it with a bit of flour. Place the parchment back on top. Flip the dough over, still keeping it between the parchment sheets, and peel off the top layer of paper.

Use a pastry wheel or sharp paring knife to trim the sides to form a square (save the scraps to re-roll). Cut the dough into 1-inch (2.5-cm) squares—you can use a ruler or just cut them free-form. Transfer the cutouts to the prepared baking sheets (they can be placed pretty close to each other since they won't spread). Use the tip of a metal skewer or toothpick to pierce a hole in the center of each cracker. Bake 9 to 10 minutes until fragrant and the edges are golden. Keep a close eye on them, as they go from done to burnt pretty quickly. Let the crackers cool on the sheet for 2 minutes, then use a small offset spatula to transfer them to a wire rack to finish cooling completely.

(recipe continues on next page)

Store the crackers in an airtight container for up to 3 days (if they even last that long—Mikey always seemed to eat them quicker than I could make them).

> **MAKE AHEAD** Place the cut-out, unbaked crackers onto a waxed paper-lined baking sheet. Place the sheet in the freezer to let the crackers flash-freeze, about 1 hour. Transfer the frozen crackers into a plastic zip-top bag. Follow the baking instructions as directed in the recipe—surprisingly, you don't need any extra time to cook the frozen ones.

COCOA-CANDIED NUTS

I bake like crazy year-round, but come Christmas time, my oven pretty much runs non-stop. There are only so many cookies and cakes one person can make, though, which is why these nuts are on heavy rotation during the holidays. They take just a few minutes to prepare, and look beautiful in clear cellophane bags tied with ribbon. I can't help thinking of Mikey when I make them because they have all the qualities he loved in a snack—crunchy, sweet, salty, and just a hint of spice.

MAKES ABOUT 8 CUPS (595 GRAMS)

½ cup (79 grams) packed light or dark brown sugar

½ cup (100 grams) granulated natural cane sugar

½ teaspoon (3 grams) sea salt

1 teaspoon (4 grams) cinnamon

1 teaspoon (3 grams) smoked paprika

2 tablespoons (14 grams) cocoa powder

1 large egg white, at room temperature

1 tablespoon (15 ml) cold water

1 pound (453 grams) assorted raw unsalted nuts

Preheat the oven to 300°F (150°C). Line a rimmed baking sheet with parchment paper or a silicone liner.

Add the sugars, salt, cinnamon, paprika, and cocoa to a bowl and stir with a fork to mix well.

In a large bowl, whisk the egg white and water until foamy but not stiff. Add the nuts and stir them until well coated. Sprinkle the sugar mixture over the nuts and toss, or stir with a rubber spatula, until evenly coated.

Spread the nut mixture into a single layer on the prepared baking sheet. Bake for 30 minutes, stirring halfway through. Remove from the oven and let the nuts cool for 10 to 15 minutes. Break up any large pieces. Store the nuts in an airtight container in a cool, dry place for up to 2 weeks.

MOVIE THEATER POPCORN

Most parents will agree that seeing a movie in a theater when it's released, and not on DVD or On Demand six months after the fact, feels like a special occasion. That means that when I do get out to the movies, I'm as excited for the concession stand as I am for the movie itself. Now, I can at least replicate part of the experience at home. I based this recipe on my favorite movie theater popcorn in New York City, sold at Film Forum.

SERVES 4

1 tablespoon (15 ml) canola oil
$^1/_2$ cup (95 grams) popcorn kernels
2 tablespoons (14 grams) unsalted butter, cut into 8 pieces
$^1/_4$ teaspoon (2 grams) fine sea salt

Add the oil and 3 kernels of popcorn to a deep 4-quart pot. Cover and place the pot over medium-high heat on the stovetop. Heat until the kernels pop: this tells you that the oil is ready to pop the rest. The oil will smoke just a bit, but don't worry. Immediately add the remaining kernels and the butter. Cover and (using pot holders) hold the pot by the handles and shake vigorously until most of the kernels have popped, 2 to 3 minutes.

Remove the pot from the heat. Carefully lift the cover, and don't hang your face over the pot—it'll be very hot and a stray kernel could pop out. Sprinkle the salt on top, cover, and shake vigorously until the popcorn is well coated. Serve immediately.

EGG-FREE V 30 MINUTES OR LESS GLUTEN-FREE

ROSEMARY & PECORINO POPCORN

After the kids went to bed, Mikey and I would often meet on the couch
for a "date." He'd usually make us tea and I'd put a snack together—popcorn was a perennial
favorite (see Movie Theater Popcorn on page 165). In this version, the rosemary adds a fragrant
flavor and aroma, balanced out by the salty sharpness of Pecorino Romano cheese. It also tastes
great with a generous pinch of freshly ground black pepper tossed in at the last minute.

SERVES 4

1 tablespoon (15 ml) extra-virgin olive oil
$^1/_2$ cup (95 grams) popcorn kernels
$^1/_4$ cup (29 grams) very finely grated Pecorino Romano cheese
5-inch (12-cm) sprig of fresh rosemary, needles removed and finely chopped
Fine sea salt

Add the oil and 3 kernels of popcorn to a deep 4-quart pot. Cover and place the pot over medium-high heat on the stovetop. Heat until the kernels pop: this tells you that the oil is ready to pop the rest. The oil will smoke just a bit, but don't worry. Immediately add the remaining kernels, cover, and (using pot holders) hold the pot by the handles and shake vigorously until most of the kernels have popped, 2 to 3 minutes.

Remove the pot from the heat. Carefully lift the cover, and don't hang your face over the pot—it'll be very hot and a stray kernel could pop out. Sprinkle the cheese and rosemary on top, cover, and shake vigorously until the popcorn is well coated. Taste and season with salt to your liking, but remember that the cheese is already salty, so it might not need much more.

SWEET CINNAMON PITA CHIPS

Mikey wasn't the only one who had a weakness for snacks in our house.
I've got a major sweet tooth, and I love crunchy snacks—talk about a double whammy. Carrot sticks only get me so far in satisfying the latter longing. For days when I need to fulfill that sweet, crunchy snack craving, these pita chips fit the bill.

SERVES 4 TO 6

2 tablespoons (30 grams) granulated natural cane sugar

1 teaspoon (4 grams) ground cinnamon

$1/4$ teaspoon (1 gram) allspice

$1/4$ teaspoon (1 gram) fine sea salt

4 (6-inch/15-cm) pita bread pockets, split in half

4 tablespoons (56 grams) unsalted butter, melted

Preheat the oven to 350ºF (180ºC).

In a small bowl, stir the sugar, spices, and salt together with a fork to mix.

Lay the pita bread halves on a cutting board. Brush them lightly with the melted butter. Sprinkle an even amount of the spice-sugar mixture on top.

Slice each half (as if you're cutting a pizza) into 8 triangles. Arrange them in a single-layer on two rimmed baking sheets. Bake for 10 minutes, until crisp and golden. Let the chips cool for at least 5 minutes before serving. These may be stored in an airtight canister for up to 2 days.

A SAVORY SPIN Turn these sweet chips into a cocktail party snack by omitting the sugar, cinnamon, and allspice, and swapping in $1/4$ cup (28 grams) grated Parmesan cheese mixed with $1/4$ teaspoon freshly ground black pepper to sprinkle on top. These Parmesan Black Pepper Pita Chips are a perfect pairing with the Roasted Broccoli Dip on page 160.

EGG-FREE MAKE AHEAD V 30 MINUTES OR LESS

BAKED POTATO CHIPS

Making homemade chips is easy, but it does require a time commitment.
You'll need to cook the chips at a low temperature to slowly dry out the liquid in the potatoes and ensure a nice crunch. I like to make these when I'm engrossed in a boring task that takes hours to finish, like cleaning out the closets. By the end of the day, I can beam with pride at my new sense of organization and enjoy a snack to go with my well-deserved glass of wine.

SERVES 2, AS A LIGHT SNACK

1 medium russet potato, sliced paper-thin
Sea salt

Preheat the oven to 225ºF (110ºC), with the racks arranged on the upper and lower thirds. Line two rimmed baking sheets with silicone mats.

Arrange the potato slices in a single layer on the sheets and sprinkle with salt. Bake for 1 hour until the slices are crisp and dried, turning the chips and rotating the trays halfway through. Let them cool on the sheet for 10 minutes before transferring to a wire rack to cool completely. These may be be made up to 2 days in advance, provided that the weather is cool and not humid. Store the chips in an airtight metal canister at room temperature.

TECH TALK Slicing 101: If you want thin, crispy chips, you'll need a good knife with a sharp edge. The first few cuts may take practice, so have an extra potato on hand for backup. Another alternative is to invest in a mandolin slicer that makes precise, paper-thin cuts. For $30 to $40, you can buy a good quality one that allows you to adjust the thickness of your cuts, making the slicer valuable for prepping recipes beyond this one.

VEGAN   GLUTEN-FREE   MAKE AHEAD

SMOKY CARAMEL CORN

One Halloween, I'd planned to make caramel corn to fill goody bags for our party, but I hadn't actually read the recipe for making it (yes, I broke one of my own cardinal rules!). With only two hours until guests would start arriving, the traditional oven method was not an option. Rather than scrap the idea and think of something else, I wondered if I could improvise with my microwave. A few Google searches gave hope that I could: it was just a matter of figuring out the cooking time, since it varies depending on the size of the microwave.

I used to make caramel corn with corn syrup as almost every recipes calls for, but I stopped using it a few years ago. That's where the brown rice syrup comes in to play, and it actually works better than the corn syrup. Brown rice syrup's honey-like consistency adds a thicker coating on the popcorn—but don't worry, you still get a crisp, crunchy bite. I also added a Mikey touch to this recipe with a bit of heat from some chipotle powder. There's a combination of sweet, salty, and spicy in every bite.

MAKES 8 CUPS (448 GRAMS)

5 tablespoons (70 grams) unsalted butter

$^1/_3$ cup (100 grams) brown rice syrup

$^2/_3$ cup (5 ounces) packed dark brown sugar

$^1/_2$ teaspoon (2.5 ml) vanilla extract

1 teaspoon (3 grams) chipotle powder

$^1/_4$ teaspoon (1 gram) baking soda

8 cups (48 grams) popped popcorn (plain or lightly salted, but not buttered)

Sea salt flakes (I use Maldon), for finishing

Line two rimmed baking sheets with silicone liners or parchment paper.

Add the butter to a deep, microwave-safe glass bowl. Cook on high power for 1 minute until melted. Stir in the brown rice syrup and sugar. Cook again on high power until the sugar is completely dissolved, about 2 minutes depending on your microwave (mine is 1000 watts).

Quickly stir in the vanilla extract, chipotle powder, and baking soda—it will bubble slightly, and that's okay. Use a rubber spatula coated with butter to fold in the popcorn, trying to coat each piece. The mixture will be very sticky. Cook on high power until the caramel coating begins to turn lightly golden, 90 seconds to 2 minutes. Carefully remove the bowl from the microwave (it will be very hot) and stir again to make sure the kernels are thoroughly coated. Cook again on high power until the coating gets a deeper golden color and the caramel corn starts to smell like butterscotch, 1 to 2 more minutes, watching carefully during the last 30 seconds to ensure it doesn't burn.

Using a rubber spatula, spread the caramel corn into a single layer on the prepared trays. Lightly sprinkle with sea salt flakes to taste. Let cool completely, about 30 minutes. Break up into pieces before serving. The caramel corn can be stored in an airtight tin for up to 3 days.

POWER MATTERS Actual cooking times vary according to your microwave's power output, which is measured in watts. This recipe was tested using a 1000-watt model. Smaller wattage ovens may require a longer cooking time, and larger ones may require less.

SNACKS

13.

Sweet TREATS

THERE WAS NO SHORTAGE OF BAKED GOODS AROUND our house when I was growing up. Boxes of Entenmann's crumb cake and chocolate frosted doughnuts were regulars in our shopping carts. Muffins and cakes usually came out of a box ready to eat, or from a mix that just needed some eggs and oil.

Come the holidays, though, my mom would haul out her stand mixer and make some of the most beautiful winter wonderlands out of gingerbread—all from scratch. As I grew up, baking became more than a special occasion event. It became my passion, and today my house is much like my mom's in that most days, there's a cake, a pie, or some cookies hanging around the counter, except now they're all 100% homemade.

SWEET BUTTER PASTRY CRUST

If forming and fluting a pie crust makes you nervous, then it's time to give free-form tarts a try. I use this dough for making family-size tarts, like the Peach Raspberry one (opposite page), and individual hand pies (page 177). My trick to a really crisp bottom on the larger tarts is preheating the baking sheet. The dough needs minimal chilling time, so when you're up to that step, stick it in the fridge and use that twenty minutes or so to prep your filling ingredients.

MAKES ONE 12-INCH TART (30-CM) OR 16 HAND PIES

1¹/₂ cups (210 grams) unbleached all-purpose flour

³/₄ teaspoon (3 grams) fine sea salt

¹/₄ cup (50 grams) granulated natural cane sugar

1¹/₂ sticks (6 ounces) cold unsalted butter, cut into 12 pieces

3 tablespoons (45 ml) ice cold water

Add the flour, salt, and sugar to a deep bowl and whisk to combine. Scatter the butter pieces over the flour mixture and use a pastry blender, two butter knives, or your fingers to cut in the butter (this can also be done in a food processor). Sprinkle the cold water over the crumbly dough and stir with a fork until the dough forms a rough ball. Wrap in plastic and let the dough rest in the refrigerator for 20 to 30 minutes until just firm enough to roll out.

> **GO SAVORY** If you are using this dough with a savory filling, just omit the sugar and follow the dough recipe as directed.

> **FREEZE IT!** I usually make a double batch of this dough—one for using the same day, and another to tuck away in the freezer. Wrap the dough tightly in two layers of plastic wrap, then store it in the freezer in a plastic zip-top bag. The day before you plan to use it, transfer the wrapped dough to the fridge and let it thaw overnight.

30 MINUTES OR LESS · PANTRY BASICS · MAKE AHEAD · V · FF

PEACH RASPBERRY TART

New York City is known as the concrete jungle for a reason. July and
August often bring triple-digit temperatures, and the humidity makes the city's air thick and
heavy. Since summer coincides with berry and peach season, I used to make this tart in secret
when Mikey wasn't home so he wouldn't think I was nuts for turning on the oven in such weather.
The pairing of peaches and raspberries is a winning combination, and is worth every bit of extra
heat I endure to make it once summer rolls around.

SERVES 8

1 batch Sweet Butter Pastry Crust (page 174)

4 peaches, peeled and sliced

1/2 pint (100 grams) raspberries

2 tablespoons (28 grams) unsalted butter, cut into 8 pieces

1/4 cup (50 grams) granulated natural cane sugar

Place a rimmed baking sheet onto the center rack of the oven. Preheat the oven to 400°F (200°C).

On a lightly floured piece of parchment paper, roll the dough out into a 16-inch (40-cm) circle.
Scatter the fruit over the dough, leaving a 4-inch (10-cm) border. Sprinkle the sugar over the fruit
and dot with the pieces of butter. Fold the dough border up and over to partially cover the fruit,
forming a crust.

Remove the baking sheet from the oven. Leaving the tart on the parchment paper, carefully place it
on the heated baking sheet. Bake for 40 to 45 minutes, or until the crust is a deep golden color and the
fruit is bubbling in the center. Let the juices set and the tart cool on the pan for at least 10 to 15 minutes before serving. It is also great served at room temperature, but is best eaten the day it is made.

HOW TO PEEL A PEACH The best way to remove the skin from a peach is to cut an "X"
on the bottom (called scoring it), then blanch it for 30 seconds in a pot of boiling water.
The skins fall off easily this way.

SWEET CHERRY PIE POCKETS

Making a whole cherry pie sometimes seems daunting because of all
the pitting involved, so I turn my attention to these little hand pies once the season strikes. In a way, I love them even more than a slice, since the sweet, juicy filling is nestled neatly in a buttery crust. If there are any leftovers, and that's a big "if," they make for a fun homemade treat to pack in my daughters' lunches.

MAKES 16 SMALL HAND PIES

7 ounces (195 grams) sweet bing cherries, pitted and cut into quarters

2 tablespoons (30 grams) granulated natural cane sugar

$1^1/_2$ teaspoons (8 grams) unbleached all-purpose flour, plus more for dusting

Pinch of fine sea salt

1 batch Sweet Butter Pastry Crust (page 174)

1 large egg, beaten with a few drops of water

Coarse natural cane sugar, for sprinkling (optional)

Preheat oven to 400ºF (200ºC). Line two rimmed 11-inch x 17-inch (27-cm x 43-cm) baking sheets with parchment paper.

Add the cherries, sugar, flour, and salt to a bowl. Stir to mix well.

On a lightly floured surface, roll the pastry dough out $^1/_8$ inch/3 mm thick. Cut out 3-inch/6.25-cm circles. It's okay to re-roll the scraps until all the dough is used up. Place the cut circles on the prepared baking sheets. Spoon 1 to $1^1/_2$ teaspoons (6 to 9 grams) of filling onto one side of each circle, making sure to leave a $^1/_4$-inch/6-mm border so you can close the pies without the filling spilling out. Fold the other half of the circle over the filling, making sure it is not spilling out the edges. Crimp the edges closed with a fork. Gently pierce the tops with the tines of a fork, or make a slit with a sharp paring knife, to create steam vents.

Brush the tops with egg wash and sprinkle with coarse sugar, if desired. Bake for 15 minutes until the tops are golden. Let the pies sit on the sheets for 2 minutes, then transfer them, using a spatula, to a wire rack to cool further. Serve warm or at room temperature.

UNDER 1 HOUR   V

FOOLPROOF PIE CRUST

How many times have you tried a pie crust recipe claiming to be the best, only to find yourself reduced to tears? Yeah, me too. The inspiration for this crust came from Mollie Cox Bryan's vinegar pie crust recipe in *Mrs. Rowe's Little Book of Southern Pie*. Vinegar has long been a secret ingredient for pie crust, but it often gets paired with shortening. I'm not a fan of processed foods, so even organic shortening doesn't appeal to me. I set out to have the best of everything. I went for an all-butter crust and added some cornmeal for texture. The result is a tender, yet crisp pie crust that's incredibly easy to roll out as soon as it's made—no chilling necessary! Now that I think about it, maybe we should call this the best pie crust ever.

MAKES TWO 9-INCH (22-CM) PIE CRUSTS

1/3 cup (50 grams) yellow cornmeal

1 1/2 cups (210 grams) unbleached all-purpose flour, plus more for dusting

1/2 teaspoon (4 grams) fine sea salt

1 teaspoon (6 grams) granulated natural cane sugar

1 cup (224 grams) very cold unsalted butter, cut into 16 pieces

1 large egg

1 1/2 teaspoons (7.5 ml) white vinegar

2 tablespoons (30 ml) ice cold water

HOMEMADE
with
Love

Add the cornmeal, flour, salt, and sugar to the bowl of a food processor. Pulse 1 to 2 times to mix well. Add the butter and pulse a few more times, until the dough forms a sandy-looking mixture, about 4 to 5 one-second pulses. Add the egg, vinegar, and water. Pulse until it forms a solid ball of dough, about 8 to 10 one-second pulses.

Dump the ball of dough out onto a well-floured counter or surface, and knead it gently once or twice.

Divide the dough into two equal pieces, wrapping one half tightly in plastic wrap if you're making a single-crust pie (see sidebar). Roll one disc of dough out into a circle large enough to fit your pie plate. Proceed with the directions for whichever pie recipe you are using.

> **FREEZE IT!** If you're using only half the recipe, wrap the remaining disc of dough tightly in two layers of plastic wrap, then store it in the freezer in a plastic zip-top bag. The day before you plan to use it, transfer the wrapped dough to the fridge and let it thaw overnight.

BROWN BUTTER PEAR-APPLE PIE

Most apple pie recipes call for cinnamon in the filling, but I realized a few years ago this was exactly why I'd never liked apple pie. I love the delicate flavor of apples once they're baked, and see no reason to mask it with such a strong spice. Instead, I decided to toss them with some browned butter, adding a toffee-like taste to the filling. While discussing recipes for this book, Kristen, my editor, suggested adding pears to the filling, and what a winning combination it turned out to be. My last trick to elevate the humble apple pie into something extraordinary—a vanilla bean–speckled crumb topping.

MAKES ONE 9-INCH (22 CM) PIE

FOR THE PIE FILLING:

4 tablespoons unsalted butter

2 golden delicious apples (about 448 grams), peeled, cored, and thinly sliced

2 ripe bartlett pears (about 448 grams), peeled, cored, and thinly sliced

$2/3$ cup (132 grams) granulated natural cane sugar

$1/2$ teaspoon (2 grams) kosher salt

3 tablespoons (28 grams) all-purpose flour

1 tablespoon freshly squeezed lemon juice (from $1/2$ a medium lemon)

FOR THE VANILLA BEAN CRUMB TOPPING:

1 cup (145 grams) unbleached all-purpose flour

$1/3$ cup (66 grams) granulated natural cane sugar

$1/4$ teaspoon (1 gram) fine sea salt

1 vanilla bean, split and seeds scraped

6 tablespoons (84 grams) unsalted butter, melted

$1/2$ batch of Foolproof Pie Crust (page 178)

Preheat the oven to 425°F with the center rack adjusted to the lower position (this helps keep the bottom of the crust crisp). To prepare the filling, melt the butter over medium heat in a small heavy-bottomed pot. Cook until it begins to brown, but not burn; it will smell nutty and fragrant. Let cool for 5 to 10 minutes. Add the apples, pears, sugar, salt, and flour to a deep bowl, and toss with a rubber spatula to coat well. Pour in the browned butter, scraping in those browned bits, too, and the lemon juice, stir well. Let sit on the counter so the juices can thicken while you prepare the filling and roll out the piecrust.

Meanwhile, prepare the crumb topping. Whisk the flour, sugar, salt and vanilla bean seeds together in a small bowl. Pour in the melted butter and stir with a fork to thoroughly mix them together, about 30 seconds. You should be able to grab a handful of the mixture and have it clump together, holding its shape. The topping may be prepared up to three days in advance, and stored in a tightly sealed zip-top bag in the fridge.

On a lightly floured counter, roll out the pie crust. Gently fold the crust in half, then in half again,

(recipe continues on next page)

and place it in a 9-inch (22-cm) pie plate. Gently unfold the crust and arrange it in a pie plate. Spoon the filling into the crust, spreading it into an even layer. Grab small handfuls of the crumb topping, and squeeze it to form a solid piece. Sprinkle the topping over the batter, by breaking the clump of crumb topping between your fingers to create some large and small bits of topping over the filling. Repeat with the remaining crumb topping, making sure to evenly cover the top of the pie.

Bake for 15 minutes, then turn the temperature down to 350ºF (180ºC) and bake for 35 to 40 minutes more, until the topping is golden and the juices are bubbly. Cover the top loosely with foil if it begins to brown too quickly. Set the pie on a wire rack and let it cool completely before serving.

CHERRY CHOCOLATE CHIP FRIENDSHIP COOKIES

Isabella had a classmate in pre-kindergarten who was allergic to eggs, which made bringing in baked goods for class events challenging, or so I thought. When it was Isabella's turn to be "Friend of the Week"—a time when students get to know more about their fellow classmates—she asked me to make chocolate chip cookies. She also insisted that they be egg-free so all her friends could enjoy them. It's amazing what we can learn from our children about the depth of love and generosity. I don't remember why I thought to try yogurt in these cookies, but thanks to Isabella's persistence, it's now my go-to easy egg substitution in baking.

MAKES 3 DOZEN COOKIES

2 cups (290 grams) unbleached all-purpose flour

1 teaspoon (4 grams) baking soda

1/2 teaspoon (3 grams) fine sea salt

1 stick (112 grams) unsalted butter

1/2 cup (65 grams) packed dark brown sugar

1/2 cup (100 grams) granulated natural cane sugar

1/2 cup (120 grams) plain yogurt

1 teaspoon (5 ml) vanilla extract

1 (12-ounce/336-gram) bag semi-sweet chocolate chips

1/2 cup (71 grams) dried sour cherries

1 cup (100 grams) walnuts, toasted and chopped

Adjust the rack to the center position and preheat the oven to 350°F (180°C). Line 3 baking sheets with parchment paper or silicone liners.

Add the flour, baking soda, and salt to a medium sized bowl, and whisk to combine.

Add the butter and sugars to the bowl of an electric mixer and beat on high speed until light and creamy, 3 to 5 minutes. Add the yogurt and vanilla extract. Beat on medium-high speed until thoroughly mixed, 1 to 2 minutes. With the mixer on low speed, slowly pour in the dry ingredients, mixing until the dough is just combined. Scrape the sides of the bowl with a rubber spatula. Stir in the chocolate chips, cherries, and walnuts.

Drop the dough by tablespoonfuls onto the prepared baking sheets. Bake until the edges are golden, 13 to 15 minutes. Remove the trays from the oven, and let the cookies cool on the trays for 2 minutes. Using a spatula, transfer the cookies to a wire rack to finish cooling completely.

BUTTER 101 A properly softened stick of butter should be pliable, meaning you can bend it slightly, without it being mushy. This is especially important when making cookies. If the butter is too soft, they might spread too much when you bake them. You can speed up the softening process by simply cutting whatever amount you need into small pieces, and setting them on a dish while you prep the rest of your ingredients.

A GOOD COOKIE I'm obsessive about perfectly baked cookies, and the only way to ensure that with a home oven is to bake one tray at a time. While it seems logical that alternating trays halfway through helps multiple trays bake evenly, heat escapes when you do. It throws off the oven temperature each time you open the door to make the switch.

DEEP CHOCOLATE CUPCAKES

These cupcakes are big on flavor, yet incredibly light in texture.

The batter comes together quickly when you use the All-Purpose Baking Mix (page 20), which means you can cure cravings quickly or be ready for school bake sales at a moment's notice (see Quicker Cupcakes sidebar). For the sake of convenience, though, I've written the recipe using regular all-purpose flour, just in case you're running low on your baking mix—consider this a helpful reminder to replenish your stock. You can serve them simply with a dusting of confectioners' sugar, but a thick slather of Chocolate Ganache (page 195) makes these cupcakes an extra-special chocolaty treat.

MAKES ONE DOZEN

HOMEMADE *with* Love

1 cup (145 grams) unbleached all-purpose flour

1 teaspoon (5 grams) baking powder

1/4 teaspoon (1 gram) baking soda

1/8 teaspoon (1 gram) fine sea salt

1/4 cup (25 grams) good-quality dark cocoa powder (I use Valrhona)

1 large egg

1/3 cup (83 ml) canola oil

3/4 cup (150 grams) granulated natural cane sugar

1 teaspoon (5 ml) vanilla extract

1/2 cup (125 ml) milk

Confectioners' sugar, Best Vanilla Buttercream (page 197), or Chocolate Ganache (page 195), to finish

Preheat the oven to 350 °F (180°C). Line a 12-cup muffin tin with paper liners.

Combine the flour, baking powder, baking soda, salt, and cocoa in a small bowl and whisk together. Add the egg, oil, and sugar to a separate bowl, and whisk together until thick and creamy, 30 seconds to 1 minute. Stir in the vanilla and the milk. Add the dry ingredients, and stir until just combined. Whisk vigorously until well mixed, about 1 minute.

Evenly spoon the batter into the prepared tin. Bake until a metal skewer comes out clean, 15 to 17 minutes. Let the cupcakes cool in the pan for 2 minutes, then transfer them to a wire rack and cool completely before finishing with confectioners' sugar or frosting.

MAKE IT DAIRY-FREE! Swap in an equal amount of soy, coconut or almond milk for the cow's milk. Frost with Dark Chocolate Glaze (page 198).

QUICKER CUPCAKES! Omit the flour, baking powder, baking soda, and salt and swap in 1 cup (150 grams) of All-Purpose Baking Mix (page 20). Follow the recipe as directed.

PISTACHIO CUPCAKES

Just a few bites are all I usually need to satisfy my sweet cravings, making cupcakes the perfect-sized dessert. Most pistachio cupcakes rely on artificial coloring and flavorings, which is why I set out to create my own recipe a few years ago. You need a very clean, dry bowl for beating egg whites, so be sure to do that step first. They'll be fine standing for a few minutes in another bowl while you prepare the rest of the batter, and, this way, you don't have to worry about cleaning the bowl twice.

MAKES ONE DOZEN

1/2 cup (63 grams) shelled raw unsalted pistachios

1 cup (145 grams) unbleached all-purpose flour

1 1/2 teaspoons (8 grams) baking powder

1/2 teaspoon (3 grams) fine sea salt

1/2 cup (125 ml) milk

1/2 teaspoon vanilla extract

1/4 teaspoon almond extract

2 large egg whites, at room temperature

4 tablespoons (56 grams) unsalted butter

1/2 cup (100 grams) granulated natural cane sugar

Preheat the oven to 350ºF (180ºC). Line a 12-cup muffin tin with paper liners.

Pulse the pistachios in the food processor briefly to break them up, then use longer 2 to 3 second pulses to grind them very finely. It will take about 1 minute.

In a medium bowl, whisk together the flour, ground pistachios, baking powder, and salt. Set aside.

Pour the milk and extracts into a small bowl and stir to combine. Set aside

In a medium bowl, beat the egg whites on high speed with an electric mixer until stiff but not dry. Scoop them out into another bowl and return the unwashed bowl to the mixer.

Beat the butter and sugar on high speed until creamy, 3 to 5 minutes. Turn the speed to low, and gradually add the flour mixture. Pour in the liquid ingredients, and beat until just mixed (at this point, the batter will be very thick: do not overbeat or it will create a tough crumb). Using a rubber spatula, gently fold in the beaten egg whites.

Evenly spoon the batter into the prepared tin. Bake for 13 to 15 minutes, or until a metal skewer comes out clean. Let the cupcakes cool in the tin for 2 minutes, then carefully transfer them to a wire rack and let them cool completely before frosting.

WALNUT FUDGE BROWNIES

There's something magical about a nut-studded fudgy brownie, and the way it can bring a smile to people's faces. This one uses a combination of melted chocolate *and* cocoa powder to pack in extra flavor.

6 ounces semisweet or bittersweet chocolate chips

1 stick (112 grams) unsalted butter, cut into pieces

1 teaspoon (5 ml) vanilla extract

$^1/_2$ cup (75 grams) unbleached all-purpose flour

$^1/_4$ cup (25 grams) good quality dark cocoa powder

1 teaspoon (3 grams) instant espresso granules

$^1/_2$ teaspoon (2 grams) sea salt

2 large eggs

$^3/_4$ cup (150 grams) granulated natural cane sugar

1 cup (100 grams) shelled walnuts, chopped (optional)

Preheat the oven to 350°F (180°C). Grease the sides and bottom of an 8-inch (20-cm) square glass baking pan.

Measure out $^1/_4$ cup (38 grams) of the chocolate chips and set aside. Add the remaining chocolate chips to a medium bowl with the butter. Microwave on high power for 60 to 90 seconds, stirring occasionally, until the chocolate and butter are melted. Be careful not to let the chocolate burn: it happens quickly. Add the vanilla extract to the bowl and stir to combine, and set aside to cool slightly.

In a small bowl, whisk together the flour, cocoa, espresso powder, and salt. Add the eggs and sugar to a separate large bowl. Whisk until they become thick and pale yellow, about 2 minutes. Whisk in the melted chocolate mixture. Using a rubber spatula, fold in the dry ingredients and remaining chocolate chips.

Pour the batter into the prepared pan. Evenly sprinkle the chopped nuts over the top, if desired, and press them very gently into the batter. Bake for 35 to 40 minutes until the center is set and the edges gently pull away from the sides of the pan. Let cool completely before cutting.

LEMON BUTTERMILK DOUGHNUTS

I first made doughnuts during Hanukkah a few years ago. Those were "raised" doughnuts, made with yeast and deep-fried. They were crisp on the outside, and light, airy tufts of dough on the inside—perfect, but not an ideal everyday treat. They also take a few hours to make since the dough needs time to rise. These baked doughnuts are ready in fifteen minutes, have a refreshing burst of lemon, and are incredibly light, both in texture and on your waistline.

MAKES 6 DOUGHNUTS

1 scant cup (130 grams) whole wheat pastry flour

$^1/_4$ cup (50 grams) granulated natural cane sugar

1 teaspoon (5 grams) baking powder

$^1/_8$ teaspoon baking soda

$^1/_4$ teaspoon (2 grams) sea salt

Freshly squeezed juice and grated zest of 1 lemon

Scant $^1/_2$ cup (110 ml) buttermilk

1 large egg

1 tablespoon (14 grams) unsalted butter, melted

Confectioners' sugar (optional)

Preheat the oven to 425°F (220°C). Grease a 6-count doughnut pan, and set aside.

In a medium bowl, whisk together the flour, sugar, baking powder, baking soda, salt, and lemon zest.

In a measuring cup, use a fork to beat the lemon juice, buttermilk, egg, and melted butter until well blended. Pour over the flour mixture and use a wooden spoon to stir together until just combined. Evenly spoon into the prepared doughnut pan and bake for 8 to 9 minutes until the doughnuts are lightly golden and spring back when touched.

Let the doughnuts cool in the pan for 2 minutes. Unmold the doughnuts and transfer them to a wire rack to cool completely. Use a small strainer to sift confectioners' sugar over the tops before serving, if desired.

NEED A CHOCOLATE FIX? Omit the lemon juice and lemon zest. Reduce the whole wheat pastry flour to $^3/_4$ cup (97 grams) and add $^1/_4$ cup (27 grams) dark cocoa powder to the flour mixture. Stir 3 tablespoons (45 ml) brewed coffee into the milk mixture, and proceed with the directions as listed in the recipe. For an extra tasty treat, dip the cooled doughnuts in the Chocolate Ganache on page 195.

CRANBERRY COFFEE CAKE

I remember the coffee cake my family used to buy from the local shop, called College Bakery. It had a thick, generous layer of crumb that we'd all sneak into the kitchen to pick at when we thought no one was looking. Here, I've decided to match the crumb with an equally irresistible cake, making both top and bottom the main attraction. Filled with cranberries and apples, it's also a nice way to pay tribute to fall's tart and fruity flavors.

MAKES ONE (13-INCH X 9-INCH/33-CM X 22-CM) PAN

COCOA-STREUSEL TOPPING

1½ cups (217 grams) unbleached all-purpose flour

¼ cup (50 grams) granulated natural cane sugar

¼ cup (65 grams) packed dark brown sugar

2 tablespoons (14 grams) cocoa powder

1 teaspoon (4 grams) allspice

1 stick (112 grams) unsalted butter, melted

COFFEE CAKE

3 cups (435 grams) unbleached all-purpose flour

½ teaspoon (4 grams) baking soda

½ teaspoon (2 grams) salt

2 teaspoons (10 grams) baking powder

1 cup unsalted butter (224 grams), at room temperature

2 cups (200 grams) granulated natural cane sugar

4 large eggs, at room temperature

1 cup (250 ml) buttermilk

2 medium apples, peeled and grated

2 cups (240 grams) fresh cranberries, coarsely chopped

Preheat the oven to 350°F (180°C). Grease the bottom and sides of a 13-inch x 9-inch (33-cm x 22-cm) baking pan.

To make the streusel topping, add the flour, sugars, cocoa powder, and allspice to a medium bowl. Use a fork to stir in the melted butter until well combined. Set aside.

To make the cake, whisk the flour, baking soda, salt, and baking powder together in a medium bowl. Set aside. Combine the butter and sugar in a separate large bowl and beat on high speed until light and fluffy, 3 to 5 minutes.

Add the eggs, one at a time, beating well after each addition. Add one third of the dry ingredients and mix on low speed until fully incorporated. Add one third of the buttermilk and mix on low speed until fully incorporated. Repeat, alternating between the dry and wet ingredients until all have been added. Beat the batter on medium-high speed for 30 seconds.

Fold in the apples and cranberries. Spread the batter into the prepared pan. Evenly sprinkle the crumb topping over the top, making sure to get that outer edge, too. Bake for 60 minutes until a metal skewer inserted comes out clean. Let the cake cool for at least 30 minutes on a wire rack before cutting.

DIY BROWN SUGAR Organic sugar is easy to find in bulk and warehouse stores, but the same doesn't hold true for organic brown sugar. Rather than pay high prices for small bags of organic brown sugar at the supermarket, you can make it yourself. It's simply molasses and granulated natural cane sugar mixed together. For light brown sugar, add 1 cup of sugar (200 grams) and 1½ teaspoons (11 grams) molasses to the bowl of a food processor. Pulse until combined, 4 to 5 pulses (scrape the sides of the bowl after 1 or 2 pulses). For dark brown sugar, increase the molasses to 1 full tablespoon (22 grams), and follow the same directions.

CHOCOLATE TRES LECHES CAKE

Taking a soft sponge cake and soaking it with three types of milk, then topping it with fresh whipped cream sounds like the best dessert ever, right? That was the case for me until my friend Bryan walked in one day and asked if I could help him figure out how to make a chocolate tres leches cake. I may have created the recipe, but Bryan is the one you should ultimately thank for this intense chocolate experience.

MAKES ONE 13-INCH X 9-INCH (33-CM X 22-CM) PAN

FOR THE CAKE:

1 cup (145 grams) unbleached all-purpose flour

³/₄ teaspoon (4 grams) baking powder

¹/₄ teaspoon (1 gram) baking soda

¹/₄ teaspoon (1 gram) fine sea salt

¹/₄ cup (25 grams) dark cocoa powder (I use Valrhona)

4 large eggs, at room temperature

1 stick (4 ounces) unsalted butter, at room temperature

³/₄ cup (150 grams) granulated natural cane sugar

1 teaspoon (5 ml) vanilla extract

FOR THE TRES LECHES TOPPING:

1 (14-ounce/397-gram) can sweetened condensed milk

1 (7-ounce/207-ml) can evaporated milk

1 cup (250 ml) milk

FOR THE WHIPPED CREAM:

3 cups (750 ml) heavy whipping cream

¹/₂ cup (100 grams) granulated natural cane sugar

Preheat the oven to 350ºF (180ºC). Grease the bottom and sides of a 13-inch x 9-inch (33-cm x 22-cm) baking pan.

In a small bowl, whisk together the flour, baking powder, baking soda, salt, and cocoa until combined. Set aside. Separate the eggs and set aside.

Beat the egg whites in a medium bowl on high speed until stiff peaks form but the whites are still glossy, not dry (2 to 3 minutes). Set aside.

Add the butter and sugar to a separate medium-sized bowl and beat on high speed until the mixture is light and fluffy, 3 to 5 minutes. Add the egg yolks and vanilla. Beat on high speed until thick and creamy, 1 to 2 minutes. Add the dry ingredients and mix on low speed until combined. The batter will be very thick at this point.

Stir one-third of the beaten egg whites into the batter to loosen it up. Gently fold in the remaining egg whites, making sure it is well blended and there are no streaks of egg white. Using a rubber spatula, gently spread the batter into the prepared pan. Bake until a metal skewer inserted in the center comes out clean, 13 to 15 minutes.

Meanwhile, prepare the tres leches topping. Pour all the milks into a large measuring cup, or a bowl with a spout, for easy pouring. Whisk them together to mix well.

To make the whipped cream, add the cream and sugar to a medium bowl. Mix on low speed for 1 minute, then increase to high speed and beat just until stiff peaks form, about 2 minutes. (Be careful not to overbeat, or you'll end up with butter.) Cover and place in the refrigerator until ready to use.

Remove the cake from the oven, and use a metal skewer or fork to poke holes all over the cake, making sure to pierce it through to the bottom. Evenly pour the tres leches mixture over the cake. Spread the whipped cream on top. Cover with plastic wrap and let the cake sit in the fridge for at least 2 hours, or overnight, to absorb the tres leches mixture before serving.

EASY CAKE SHORTCUT Omit the flour, baking powder, baking soda and salt, and whisk in 1 cup (150 grams) of the All-Purpose Baking Mix (page 20) with the cocoa powder. Follow the directions as listed above.

DIY BAKING POWDER It's happened to the best of us. You open the cupboard and reach for the baking powder, only to realize you used up the last of it. If you have baking soda, cream of tartar, and cornstarch on hand, here's a quick fix: Whisk together 1 teaspoon (6 grams) baking soda, 1 teaspoon (4 grams) cornstarch, and 2 teaspoons (8 grams) cream of tartar. You'll have 4 teaspoons of baking powder, which should hold you over until your next supermarket run.

GOLDEN VANILLA BIRTHDAY CAKE

These directions may seem contrary to everything you've been told about making cakes. The wet and dry ingredients are added all at once, and the batter is beaten on high speed—something we've all been told is a no-no if you want tender, airy cakes. Well, just trust me here and you'll be rewarded with the most moist, buttery crumb imaginable.

MAKES TWO 8-INCH CAKE LAYERS

3¼ cups (471 grams) unbleached all-purpose flour

1 tablespoon (15 grams) baking powder

¾ teaspoon (5 grams) sea salt

2 teaspoons (10 ml) vanilla extract

1¾ cups (437 ml) milk

2 sticks (8 ounces/224 grams) unsalted butter, at room temperature

1¼ cups (250 grams) granulated natural cane sugar

4 large eggs, at room temperature

The Best Vanilla Buttercream (page 197)

Preheat the oven to 350°F. Grease the bottom and sides of two 8-inch cake pans. Place an 8-inch circle of parchment paper in the bottom of each pan. Lightly flour the sides of each pan and set aside.

In a small bowl, whisk together the flour, baking powder, and salt until combined; set aside.

In a small measuring cup, whisk the milk and vanilla together until combined; set aside.

In a large bowl, beat the butter and sugar until light and fluffy, 3 to 5 minutes. Add the eggs and beat again until light and fluffy. Scrape down the sides of the bowl with a rubber spatula.

Pour in the milk and flour mixtures, and starting on low speed, mix until all the ingredients are just combined. Turn the speed up to high and beat for 10 seconds. Scrape down sides and beat for 10 more seconds.

Evenly spoon the batter into the prepared cake pans. Gently tap the bottom of the pans on the counter to remove any air bubbles. Bake, side by side on the center rack of the oven, for 32 to 35 minutes, until tops are golden and a metal skewer inserted in the center comes out clean. Transfer the pans to a wire rack and cool completely before frosting with buttercream frosting.

WHY ROOM TEMPERATURE? For a tender, light cake, room-temperature ingredients are a must. Adding cold eggs can result in a curdled batter. Generally 20 to 30 minutes is enough time to bring eggs to the correct temperature, but if you decide to bake spur of the moment, add the uncracked eggs to a bowl filled with warm (not hot) water for about 10 minutes before you begin baking.

PUMPKIN APPLE CAKE

As I set out to bake a batch of Deep Chocolate Cupcakes (page 182)
to bring to my friend's house, I remembered that her 8-year-old daughter, Lucie, loves pumpkin and apple—muffins, cupcakes, she even made me a quick bread once! I immediately switched gears, and made a dessert inspired by Lucie. If you're like Lucie and prefer pumpkin even for your birthday cake, The Best Vanilla Buttercream on page 197 is a wonderful pairing—we taste-tested the combo just to be sure!

MAKES 10 TO 12 SERVINGS

2 cups (240 grams) whole wheat pastry flour

$^1/_2$ teaspoon (3 grams) fine sea salt

$^1/_4$ teaspoon (1 gram) baking soda

1 teaspoon (5 grams) baking powder

2 large eggs (100 grams)

$^3/_4$ cup (150 grams) granulated natural cane sugar

$^1/_4$ cup (62 ml) canola oil

1 cup (232 grams) pumpkin purée

$^1/_2$ cup (125 ml) buttermilk

1 large apple, peeled and grated

Confectioners' sugar, for dusting (optional)

Preheat the oven to 350ºF (180ºC). Grease and flour the bottom and sides of a 9-inch (22-cm) springform pan.

In a medium bowl, whisk together the flour, salt, baking soda, and baking powder to combine. Add the eggs, sugar, and oil to a separate large bowl, and whisk vigorously until thick and creamy, 1 to 2 minutes. Whisk in the pumpkin. Add the dry ingredients to the bowl and stir until it is just combined, and there are no visible traces of flour. Stir in the buttermilk. Gently fold in the apples.

Spoon the batter into the prepared pan, gently spreading it to the edges. Bake until the top is golden and a metal skewer inserted in the center comes out clean, 40 to 45 minutes. Remove from the oven and set the pan on a wire rack to cool completely. You can speed up the cooling process by carefully removing the springform pan's outer ring from the base.

To serve, dust with confectioners' sugar, if desired.

WASTE NOT, WANT NOT You'll probably have half a can of pumpkin purée left over—don't toss it. Transfer it to a small, tightly sealed container, and store it in the fridge for up to 1 week, or in the freezer for up to 1 month (thaw it in the fridge overnight before using).

SPICE IT UP Fragrant fall spices are a popular pairing with pumpkin desserts. I opted for spice-free to let the earthy flavor of the pumpkin shine through. Feel free to add $^3/_4$ teaspoon of ground cinnamon or allspice to the flour mixture before adding it to the batter.

V

CHOCOLATE GANACHE

After your first time making ganache, you'll be wondering where it's been your whole life. It's a chameleon of sorts, perfect as the base for homemade hot chocolate, as a thin icing for cupcakes, or as a thick, fudgy frosting for layer cakes.

MAKES ABOUT 2 CUPS (400 GRAMS)

10 ounces (283 grams) bittersweet chocolate chips

1 cup (250 ml) heavy whipping cream

$^3/_4$ cup (150 grams) granulated natural cane sugar

1 teaspoon (5 ml) vanilla extract

Place the chocolate chips in a glass bowl. Combine the cream and sugar in a small pot and cook until just before it reaches the boiling point, and the sugar has melted, about 5 minutes. Pour the hot cream mixture over the chocolate chips, and add the vanilla. Let it sit for 2 minutes.

Using a rubber spatula, stir until the mixture is smooth and all the chocolate has melted. Let the ganache cool 1 to 2 more minutes, if using as a glaze. You can then dip the cupcake tops into the bowl and set them on a wire rack until the glaze sets, about 20 to 30 minutes. To use the ganache as a thick frosting, place the bowl in the fridge and stir it every 30 minutes until it is thick and spreadable, about 2 hours.

The hardened ganache can also be scooped and stirred into steamed milk for a homemade hot chocolate. The ganache will keep in the fridge, stored in a tightly sealed container, for up to 1 month.

EGG-FREE MAKE AHEAD V GLUTEN-FREE

THE BEST VANILLA BUTTERCREAM

I know saying any recipe is the best is a big promise (see my pie crust on page 178, too), but this frosting delivers. Most buttercreams are cloyingly sweet—not this one. It has just enough sugar to make it worthy of icing a birthday cake, but not so much that you can't finish eating a whole slice.

MAKES 3 CUPS (637 GRAMS)

3 sticks (12 ounces/336 grams) unsalted butter, at room temperature

2^1/$_4$ cups (294 grams) confectioners' sugar

1^1/$_2$ teaspoon (7.5 ml) vanilla extract

3 tablespoons (45 ml) heavy whipping cream

Add the butter to a large bowl and beat on high with an electric mixer until fluffy, about 1 minute. Add the sugar and vanilla. Start out mixing on low speed until all of the sugar is incorporated, 1 to 2 minutes. Increase the speed to high and beat until very light and fluffy, about 2 minutes. Add the cream, and beat on high for 4 minutes more. Use immediately, or store in a tightly covered container, in a cool dry place, for up to two days. Stir vigorously with a butter knife or offset spatula to fluff the frosting back up before using.

TO DYE FOR Sometimes plain white frosting just won't do. Before committing your whole batch to a shade, use a half cup as a tester to figure out how many drops you need to get the color you want. When it comes to food coloring, I prefer the gel types, because a little goes a long way and they don't water down or affect the flavor of the frosting. If you have sensitivity to (or don't feel comfortable using) artificial dyes, check out your local health food store for all-natural options.

V   MAKE AHEAD   GLUTEN-FREE   30 MINUTES OR LESS

DARK CHOCOLATE GLAZE

Remember earlier in this chapter, when I mentioned that Isabella had a classmate allergic to eggs? Well, she also has a friend, Oliver, who's allergic to cow's milk, and to all dairy products made from it. I set out to make a chocolate glaze that had the same qualities as my chocolate ganache, but that would also be safe for Oliver to eat. I succeeded with this rich, chocolate glaze that also happens to be dairy free.

MAKES 1 CUP (210 GRAMS)

$1/2$ cup (100 grams) granulated natural cane sugar
1 cup (150 grams) bittersweet chocolate chips or discs
$1/2$ teaspoon vanilla extract

Add the sugar and $1/2$ cup (150 ml) water to a 2-quart pot. Bring to a boil over high heat. Reduce the heat to low and cook until the sugar has completely dissolved and turns into a simple syrup, about 2 minutes.

Add the chocolate to a medium glass bowl. Pour the simple syrup over the chocolate, and let it sit for 1 minute. Add the vanilla extract and whisk until it becomes a thin, smooth glaze. Pour the glaze into a glass jar and let it sit on the counter until completely cooled (it will thicken as it cools, don't worry). When the glaze is cooled, tightly seal the jar and store it in the fridge. It will harden while refrigerated. To use, scoop the amount you need into a microwave-safe bowl and microwave in 10-second intervals until it reaches the desired consistency.

> **PLAY IT SAFE** Dark and bittersweet chocolates are generally made without milk, but it's important to read your labels. These products are often manufactured in the same facility as milk chocolate. Look for chocolate that is specifically labeled dairy free to ensure there has been no cross contamination.

VEGAN · MAKE AHEAD · 30 MINUTES OR LESS

STRAWBERRY BLENDER SHERBET

I may be dating myself with this recipe, since I rarely see sherbet on menus anymore. When I was growing up, it was also labeled "ice milk," and aptly named, because it was an ice cream-like dessert that didn't contain any cream. It has a lighter consistency, and in this case it doesn't have any eggs, either. It's also one of the quickest and easiest summer desserts to make. Just prepare it ahead of time to allow a few hours for it to firm up in the freezer.

MAKES 2 CUPS (320 GRAMS)

2 cups (224 grams) frozen strawberries
$^1/_4$ cup (62 ml) simple syrup (page 203)
$^1/_2$ cup (125 ml) milk

Combine the strawberries, syrup, and milk in a blender. Blend until mostly smooth, about 3 to 5 minutes; it's okay if there are a few small chunks. Transfer to a tightly sealed container and freeze until firm, 4 to 6 hours, stirring every 1 to 2 hours.

30 MINUTES OR LESS · V · EGG-FREE · MAKE AHEAD

199

SWEET TREATS

14.

Drinks

HAVE YOU EVER WONDERED HOW TO MAKE THE BEST Homemade Pink Lemonade (page 202) or a Chocolate Egg Cream (page 207), a real Brooklyn treat? Did you know you can purée watermelon in a blender and use the juice to make a fun spritzer with fresh cilantro (page 210)? Yes, the world of homemade beverages is an endless one, and an important reminder that beverages can be loads of fun without a drop of alcohol.

HOMEMADE PINK LEMONADE

Like many little girls, Isabella and Virginia love anything pink, so one day I decided to add some strawberry purée to my homemade lemonade for a natural deep rosy color. Lemonade also happened to be Mikey's favorite beverage, and he often added a splash of seltzer to his glass for a fizzy sparkling drink.

MAKES 6½ CUPS (1.5 L)

1 pint (about 200 grams) strawberries, hulled
1 cup (250 ml) freshly squeezed lemon juice (from 4 large lemons)
½ cup Simple Syrup, plus more to taste (opposite page)

Add the strawberries to the bowl of a food processor, and process until they become a smooth purée. Pour the purée through a fine sieve to remove the seeds, using a spoon to push down the mixture and extract as much juice as possible. You should have about ¾ cup (187 ml) when you're done.

Combine the strawberry purée, lemon juice, and simple syrup with 4½ cups (1.1 L) of water in an 8-cup (2-L) pitcher. Stir well to mix. Taste to see if the lemonade is sweet enough for your liking, adding more simple syrup a tablespoon at a time, if necessary. Refrigerate until well chilled before serving, 2 to 4 hours.

> **MAKE AHEAD** The lemonade is best served the day it's made, but the individual ingredients may be prepared up to two days in advance and stored in the fridge in tightly sealed containers. By doing your prep ahead of time, and using very cold water, you'll be able to skip the chilling time and serve the lemonade immediately.

> **GET MORE FOR YOUR MONEY** Lemons, and all citrus fruits for that matter, benefit from a vigorous roll with the palm of your hand across the counter before juicing. This helps extract as much juice as possible.

SIMPLE SYRUP

It's called simple syrup for a reason—all you need is sugar and water to make it. Keep a jar in the fridge and you'll be ready to naturally sweeten homemade iced tea, lemonade, and iced coffee.

MAKES 1¼ CUPS (284 ML)

1 cup (200 grams) granulated natural cane sugar

Combine the sugar with 1 cup (250 ml) water in a small pot. Bring to a boil over medium heat, stirring occasionally to help dissolve the sugar. Once the sugar is completely dissolved, continue to cook the syrup at a rolling boil for 1 more minute. Remove the pot from the stove and set aside to cool completely. Transfer to a clean glass jar, cover, and store in the fridge for up to 1 month.

COLD-BREWED ICED TEA

The first time I made cold-brewed coffee, I was instantly hooked on the noticeably purer taste. The technique is much easier than it sounds and doesn't require any fancy gadgets. When I decided to try and kick my coffee habit a few years ago, I figured I could use my same cold-brew technique with tea bags. You simply let your tea steep for a lengthy period of time in room-temperature water, then dilute it with cold water. My coffee-free reign lasted ever so briefly, but this iced tea is still a regular in my summer drink rotation.

MAKES 4 CUPS (1 L)

6 black tea bags
Simple Syrup, to taste (see recipe, above)
Lemon wedges, for garnish (optional)

Add the tea bags and 1 cup (250 ml) of room-temperature water to a glass pitcher. Push the tea bags to the bottom of the glass until they absorb some of the water and don't float to the top. Let the tea bags "brew" for 6 to 8 hours at room temperature. Remove the tea bags from the pitcher but do not squeeze them, as this makes for a bitter-tasting tea.

(recipe continues on next page)

Add 3 cups (750 ml) of cold water and the simple syrup, if desired. Stir to mix well. Serve over ice, with a wedge of lemon, if desired. Iced tea may be stored in a covered container in the fridge for up to 3 days.

MAKE IT YOUR OWN You can use this method of making iced tea with any of your favorite flavors. In fact, I usually make mine decaffeinated so the kids can enjoy it without the extra buzz.

ITALIAN COFFEE SODA

Opening an icy-cold bottle of Manhattan Special, an espresso coffee soda, was a rite of passage growing up in Carroll Gardens, Brooklyn. Even better was having a frothy mug of it straight from the tap at Ferdinando's, a little Sicilian restaurant that's been in the neighborhood for over a hundred years. A few years ago, word on the street was that the company that manufactures Manhattan Special was in danger of going out of business. I didn't know if there was any truth to that rumor, but I wasn't taking any chances. I marched into my own kitchen and started playing with ratios to make it at home. The soda is still readily available, but I've got my backup plan—just in case.

MAKES 1 SERVING

1/2 cup (125 ml) espresso, cooled completely (see sidebar)
1 to 2 teaspoons (5 to 10 ml) Simple Syrup (page 203), or more to taste
1/2 cup (125 ml) seltzer, from a freshly opened bottle

Add the espresso and simple syrup to a 12-ounce glass, and stir to combine. Fill the glass with ice, then pour in the seltzer. Be prepared for it to foam up a bit: that's what the extra head space is for in the glass. Serve immediately.

DIY ESPRESSO Nothing beats a properly brewed shot of espresso if you're drinking it straight, but not having a machine or special equipment shouldn't stand between you and this homemade coffee soda. Simply brew your normal coffee (French press, stove-top, or coffeemaker) at a triple strength, meaning you should use *three times* the amount of ground coffee during the brewing process (the water amount stays the same).

COFFEE FRAPPÉ

Mikey was usually a "coffee black with one sugar" kind of guy, but on a hot summer day he couldn't resist the allure of a Frappuccino from Starbucks. It was with that in mind that I created this frosty coffee drink for him to enjoy. It took a few tries to get the recipe just right, but it was a taste-test challenge he was all too happy to take on in the name of love. He saved quite a few bucks, too, since these cost a lot less to make at home.

MAKES 2 SERVINGS

$^1/_2$ cup (125 ml) triple-strength coffee, cooled completely (see sidebar on page 204)
$^1/_4$ cup (62 ml) milk
1 to 2 tablespoons (18 to 36 grams) granulated natural cane sugar, or more to taste
$1^1/_2$ cups (336 grams) ice cubes

Add all the ingredients to a blender. Blend well until it is frothy and the ice is crushed into very fine bits, about 90 seconds. Evenly divide the frappé between two glasses, and serve immediately.

MAKE IT A MOCHA! Add 1 tablespoon (15 ml) of Homemade Chocolate Syrup (page 234) to the blender before blending the ingredients.

CHOCOLATE EGG CREAM

To answer your first question, no, there isn't any egg in this drink, though recipes from the late nineteenth century suggest that there used to be. As for your next question—why is it called an egg cream? Well, that's an answer no one really knows. There's lots of speculation, but the one thing everyone can agree on is that this spritzy chocolate milk drink has strong roots in Brooklyn. My mom grew up drinking it, I grew up drinking it, and now my girls—third-generation Brooklynites—love it, too.

MAKES 1 SERVING

¹⁄₄ cup (62 ml) milk
1 teaspoon (5 ml) Homemade Chocolate Syrup (page 234)
¹⁄₂ cup (125 ml) seltzer, from a freshly opened bottle

Add the milk and chocolate syrup to a 10-ounce (300-ml) glass. Stir well to combine. Vigorously stir the milk mixture with a spoon as you slowly pour in the seltzer. It will foam up considerably, forming a foamy "head"—this is the signature look of an egg cream. Sip and enjoy!

MAKE IT DAIRY FREE Don't let a sensitivity or an allergy to dairy stop you from enjoying an egg cream. Just swap in soy milk for a dairy-free treat. Almond and coconut milk work well, too, just be prepared for a flavored experience, as these impart a nutty or coconut taste.

V · 30 MINUTES OR LESS · EGG-FREE · GLUTEN-FREE · DAIRY-FREE ADAPTABLE

BLUEBERRY-LEMON SPRITZER

This was originally supposed to be a recipe for blueberry soda, but as I opened the freezer to grab some ice cubes, my eyes wandered to a bag of lemon ice cubes. Now, I realize not everyone has lemon ice cubes hanging out in their freezer, but trust me: they're so easy a 3-year-old can make them, especially if your little ones love squeezing lemons as much as mine does.

MAKES 1 SERVING

4 lemon ice cubes (see sidebar)

Ice cubes to a fill a 10-ounce glass

6 ounces (180 ml) seltzer, from a freshly opened bottle

2 tablespoons (46 grams) Homemade Blueberry Syrup (page 220)

Add the lemon and plain ice cubes to a 10-ounce (300-ml) glass. Pour in the seltzer. Stir in the blueberry syrup. It's okay if some bits of blueberry are floating in there. They make the drink look pretty and are a fun treat to nibble on when you've finished sipping the soda.

EASY LEMON ICE CUBES When life gives you a recipe that only calls for lemon zest, it's a good excuse to make lemon ice cubes. I keep a tray in my freezer for just this purpose, and refill it with more juice as I go along. Once the cubes have frozen, transfer them to a tightly sealed plastic zip-top bag so they stay fresh.

VEGAN 30 MINUTES OR LESS GLUTEN-FREE

WATERMELON-CILANTRO SPARKLER

Years ago I started making watermelon-cilantro margaritas—they're the perfect summer cocktail for barbecues. They're not exactly a kid-friendly drink, though, so I created this alcohol-free sparkler as a fun, refreshing thirst-quencher that everyone could enjoy.

SERVES 4

4 ounces (113 grams) watermelon, diced (about 1 cup)

Freshly squeezed juice of 1 lime

2 tablespoons (30 ml) Simple Syrup (page 203)

Handful of fresh cilantro

Freshly opened 33-ounce (1-L) bottle of seltzer

4 lime wedges or small watermelon wedges, for garnish (optional)

Add the diced watermelon to a food processor or mini chopper. Pulse until puréed.

Add the watermelon purée, lime juice, simple syrup, cilantro, and 6 ice cubes to a cocktail shaker. Shake vigorously for 30 seconds.

Fill four rocks glasses with ice. With the strainer in place on the cocktail shaker, pour an even amount into each glass. There will be fine bits of cilantro in the drink, and this is fine. Top the glasses off with seltzer and garnish each with a wedge of lime or watermelon, if desired. Serve immediately.

VEGAN 30 MINUTES OR LESS GLUTEN-FREE

15.

Jams, Salsas
& CONDIMENTS

CANNING HAS BECOME SUCH AN IMPORTANT PART OF my life, and something I thought was strictly for country folk until a few years ago—how silly is that? The pure enjoyment of taking raw ingredients and putting them up for the off-season is easy enough for anyone to do, regardless of geographic location or kitchen size. Imagine slathering a taste of summer in the form of homemade strawberry jam (page 217) onto toast during the coldest of winter days. That's the reward you can enjoy if you do a little advance planning as soon as those bright red berries become available at your local farmers' market.

My favorite experiment to date has been pickled watermelon rind. One day, as I watched the rinds pile up while the kids gnawed away at each piece, I sighed, swearing to start a compost bin. As I stared at those rinds, the texture started reminding me of cucumbers—I was in my second year of making pickles. Turns out I stumbled onto a real Southern treat, and gave it my own spin with allspice berries and jalapeños (page 224). The compost bin is still on my to-do list.

Then there are those items you've probably been buying prepackaged all your life, and wonder if they're worth the time it takes to make from scratch. In the case of mayonnaise (page 229) and whole grain mustard (page 227), one taste and you'll know the answer is undoubtedly yes.

BASIC TRAINING: CANNING 101

First, I should preface that putting food up for long-term storage is an extensive topic, which is why there are whole sections devoted to it in bookstores. My basic training tips are meant to help you gently ease into the world of preserving and pickling. For that reason, my canning suggestions are limited to the hot-water bath method because it involves minimal investment to get started. Pressure canning, on the other hand, requires a special type of pot, which is a costly investment, especially if you're not sure canning is the "thing" for you just yet (although I bet you'll be an instant convert!). Pressure canners are also pretty large, posing storage issues for cramped city dwellers.

But back to the hot water method: Ball has a great product for beginners called the Ball Canning Discovery Kit (at the time of writing this book it costs only $10 on Amazon.com). This is not a paid endorsement—I really love how this kit makes canning a breeze! It includes an easy-to-store, heatproof plastic basket that makes placing the jars in hot water, and then removing them, very safe and efficient. The only other item you need, aside from the canning jars and lids, is something you likely already have—a large stock pot.

Canning Checklist

- Clean, sterilized glass canning jars
- Clean, sterilized lids and rings (the type varies depending on the kind of jar you use)
- 8-quart (7.5-liter) stock pot, with a removable rack in the bottom*
- Canning tongs* (these are rubber coated and wider than cooking tongs, allowing you to safely remove the jars from the boiling water).

*This item is included in the canning kit I mentioned.

Hot Water Bath Canning

1. Fit an 8-quart (7.5-liter) stock pot with a rack in the bottom. This elevates the jars so they don't come into direct contact with the pot, which may cause them to break from the heat. You can skip this step if you're using the plastic canning basket.

2. Fill the pot with water to about 6 inches (15 cm) below the rim (you need to leave room so the water doesn't overflow when you add the jars to the pot). Bring the water to a rolling boil and add the clean, empty jars using canning tongs.

3. Once your recipe is finished and ready to process, remove the jars from the hot water and set them gently on a kitchen towel-lined counter. Fill them with the recipe while everything is still hot, leaving ½ inch of headspace. Top the jars with the lids and seal with rings, taking care not to overtighten. The rings should be "fingertip tight:" no tighter than you can easily screw on with your fingers.

4. Immediately and carefully place the jars back in the boiling water, and rest them on the rack or in the basket. They should be covered by at least an inch or two of water. If you try to add cold jars or jars filled with cold contents to the hot water, they could crack from the change in temperature.

5. Let the water come back to a boil, and at this point you can start the clock for your processing time. This is the amount of time it takes to make the item you are canning shelf stable for long-term storage.

6. Once the processing time is complete, carefully remove the jars from the water. Place them on a heatproof counter. As they sit on the counter and start to cool down, you will begin to hear a popping sound—this means success! The popping sound indicates that the air has been completely released from the jar, creating a vacuum seal between the lid and the jar itself. The lid should also have decompressed, so you should not be able to push it in with your finger.

> **NOTE:** If a lid is still raised, and you don't hear a pop, it's possible the sealant around the lid was faulty. You will need to open the jar, fit it with a new lid, and start the canning process again from Step 1 to be sure your food is safe for long term storage. Don't get too worried or anxious about this "if." In my four years of canning, I've had very few "bum" lids—most seal perfectly the first time around!

SWEET & SAVORY TOMATO JAM

The first time I made this, I dumped all the ingredients into a pot and puttered around the house doing chores. I checked in periodically, but not obsessively. Keep that in mind when making it the first time. Too much checking and stirring will cause worry, because it stays a very soupy consistency until the last 20 to 30 minutes when it starts to thicken up properly—just trust me here.

MAKES 3 PINTS (675 GRAMS)

3¹/₂ pounds (1.6 kg) tomatoes, coarsely chopped

1 small yellow onion, diced

¹/₂ cup (79 grams) packed dark brown sugar

1¹/₂ cups (300 grams) granulated natural cane sugar

1 teaspoon (6 grams) fine sea salt

¹/₄ teaspoon (1 gram) ground coriander

¹/₄ teaspoon ground cumin

¹/₄ cup (62 ml) apple cider vinegar

Freshly squeezed juice of 1 lemon

1 small tart green apple, cored and finely diced

Combine all the ingredients in a 2-quart pot. Bring to a gentle boil, then reduce the heat to a simmer. Cook, stirring occasionally, until it becomes a thickened, jam-like consistency that coats the back of a spoon, about 3 hours. Transfer to sterilized glass jars and store in the fridge for up to 2 weeks, or process in a hot-water bath for 15 minutes for long-term storage in your dry goods pantry (page 215).

THE EASIEST STRAWBERRY JAM EVER

Making strawberry jam was my first foray into preserving. I was blown away by the first spoonful, but the defining moment was when I opened a jar of my homemade stuff the following winter. Nary a fresh or local berry was to be had, but canning my own jam transported me back to the warm May days of the spring before. I knew there was no turning back.

Since then, I've made jam on the stovetop, but nothing beats the ease and speed of the microwave, especially when little ones are always underfoot. Pomona's Universal Pectin is available in larger supermarkets and health food stores, and requires a lot less sugar for the jam to set up, compared to other commercial pectins—this means you really get to taste the fruit without cloying sweetness.

MAKES ABOUT 3 CUPS (350 GRAMS)

2 pints (about 400 grams) strawberries, hulled

2 teaspoons (10 ml) calcium water (included with pectin package)

2 teaspoons (10 ml) Pomona's Universal Fruit Pectin

1 cup (200 grams) granulated natural cane sugar

In a large glass microwave-safe bowl, mash the berries to your desired consistency depending on whether you prefer a smooth or chunky jam. A potato masher does the job perfectly. Stir in the calcium water. Cook on high in the microwave until the berries are almost boiling, about 6 minutes.

Meanwhile, whisk the pectin powder into the sugar. Using a wooden spoon, stir the sugar mixture into the berries. Return the bowl to the microwave and cook on high for 3 more minutes, until the jam is slightly thickened and clings to the back of a spoon.

Ladle the jam into clean, sterilized glass jars and store in the refrigerator, once completely cooled, for up to 3 weeks, or process in a hot water bath for 10 minutes for long-term storage in your dry goods pantry (page 215).

TECH TALK All microwaves aren't created equal, so keep in mind that cooking times will vary with different models. The times listed here are based on a 1000-watt microwave.

APRICOT BUTTER

I wasn't in a big baking mood the first Christmas after Mikey passed away, but that didn't mean I was giving up hope on homemade holiday gifts for the friends who held my hand through a very tough year of firsts. I turned to a pantry staple my daughters love eating—dried apricots. I had a hunch they would transform into a lovely "butter" with a quick poach in another household staple—plain ol' water. I skipped adding sugar, since dried apricots have a concentrated sweetness, and a little bit of vanilla extract added a subtle nuance to the flavor. It's perfect for slathering on toast, stirring into yogurt, or enjoying straight from the spoon as my dear friend Erin likes to do.

MAKES 1½ PINTS (300 GRAMS)

8 ounces (226 grams) dried apricots
¼ teaspoon vanilla extract

Combine the apricots and vanilla with 1¼ cups (312 ml) of water in a 2-quart pot and bring to a boil over medium-high heat. Reduce to a simmer, with just a few gentle bubbles popping to the surface, and cook until the apricots are plump and half the water has been absorbed, 15 to 20 minutes.

Remove the pot from the stove and set it aside to let the apricots cool completely. Once cooled, add the apricots and their cooking liquid to the bowl of a food processor (if using a mini-chopper, you may have to do this step in two batches). Pulse a few times to break down the apricots, then run the processor on a steady stream until it forms a smooth mixture, 1 to 2 minutes. Spoon into clean sterilized jars and store in the fridge for 3 to 4 weeks, or process in a hot water bath for 10 minutes to preserve for long-term storage in your dry goods pantry (page 215).

BOOZY APRICOT BUTTER Make a grown-up butter by swapping 2 tablespoons of the water for Grand Marnier or other orange liqueur.

219
JAMS,
SALSAS &
CONDI
MENTS

Apricot Butter (left) and The Easiest Strawberry Jam Ever (right), page 217

HOMEMADE BLUEBERRY SYRUP

I've seen plenty of recipes for blueberry syrup made by simply simmering blueberries in a pot with maple syrup. While that method produces a tasty topping for pancakes and waffles, I wanted to create a syrup that would be more versatile—no one-hit wonders here! In this recipe, the blueberries cook down into a truly homemade syrup by just simmering with water, sugar, and a whisper of almond extract in a pot on the stovetop. The result is an intensely fruity syrup that can be used on your favorite breakfast dishes, on ice cream, and even to make homemade soda (like the Blueberry-Lemon Spritzer on page 208).

MAKES 1¼ CUPS (460 GRAMS)

2 cups (196 grams) frozen wild blueberries
½ cup (100 grams) granulated natural cane sugar
¼ teaspoon pure almond extract

Add the blueberries, sugar, and almond extract plus ½ cup (125 ml) of water to a 2-quart pot and bring to a boil over medium-high heat. Reduce to a simmer, with just a few gentle bubbles popping on the surface. Cook until the blueberry mixture reduces by about one third, about 20 minutes.

Remove the pot from the stove and set aside to let it cool completely. Store in a tightly sealed glass jar in the fridge for up to 1 month. If using on pancakes or waffles, heat the desired amount in a small pot on the stovetop or in the microwave until it is warmed through.

SHOPPING TIP Check your local warehouse club like Costco for frozen wild blueberries in bulk. I stock up on a 5-pound bag every couple of months.

ROASTED RHUBARB JAM

This is seriously the easiest jam recipe you'll ever make. No pectin, no need for constant stirring, and you only need three ingredients. If you're still wondering about the merits of making your own jam, this is the recipe to get you started. Usually rhubarb requires more sugar than seems socially acceptable—it's a particularly acidic fruit (actually, it's really a vegetable). Roasting it helps tame the flavor, allowing you to get by with a little less sugar than you might need for a traditional stovetop recipe.

MAKES 1 GENEROUS CUP (250 GRAMS)

1 pound (453 grams) rhubarb, tough ends trimmed, cut into large chunks
$^1/_2$ cup (100 grams) granulated natural cane sugar
$^1/_4$ teaspoon cinnamon

Preheat the oven to 400ºF (200ºC). Toss the rhubarb together with the sugar and cinnamon in a 9-inch x 13-inch (22-cm x 33-cm) nonstick baking dish. Roast for 20 minutes until thick and bubbly, stirring halfway through. Remove the pan from the oven and let the rhubarb cool completely. Transfer to a tightly sealed jar and store in the fridge for up to 2 weeks.

SAME-DAY PICKLES

Most pickle recipes call for soaking cucumbers in cold water overnight
to crisp them up. I've never been known for my patience, so I dodge that theory by selecting super fresh and crisp kirby cucumbers in the springtime at the farmers' market. The key is to make these pickles the day you buy the cucumbers, since they lose their crispness very quickly.

MAKES 1 QUART (494 GRAMS)

4 cups (400 grams) thinly sliced kirby cucumbers (from about 6 cucumbers)

1 small yellow onion, thinly sliced

2 tablespoons (36 grams) fine sea salt

2 cups (500 ml) apple cider vinegar

$1\frac{1}{2}$ cups (300 grams) granulated natural cane sugar

2 teaspoons (10 grams) mustard seeds

$\frac{1}{4}$ teaspoon dried allspice berries

$\frac{1}{4}$ teaspoon celery seeds

$\frac{1}{2}$ teaspoon coriander seeds

HOMEMADE *with* *Love*

Add the cucumber and onion slices to a deep bowl. Sprinkle with the salt, toss well, and let sit for 30 minutes. Transfer the cucumbers and onions to a strainer and rinse under cold water until all the salt has washed away.

Meanwhile, add the vinegar and sugar to a 4-quart (4.5-L) pot over medium-high heat. Bring to a boil, then reduce the heat to a simmer and cook for 5 minutes. Add the spices along with the cucumber and onion. Raise the heat to return the mixture to a boil once more, then reduce the heat to a simmer and cook for 3 more minutes. Do not overcook, or you'll end up with limp pickles. Transfer the pickles and brine to clean glass jars and process the jars in a hot water bath for 10 minutes for long term storage (page 215). To use right away, let the jars cool and store them in the fridge—the pickles are ready to eat as soon as they're chilled, 3 to 4 hours. They will keep in the fridge for up to 2 months.

Clockwise from top: Sweet and Savory Tomato Jam (page 216),
Jalapeño Pickled Watermelon Rind (page 224), Same-Day Pickles

JALAPEÑO PICKLED WATERMELON RIND

Mikey loved watermelon, and our daughters follow in his footsteps.
My favorite part about watermelon season is getting to make these spicy, crunchy pickles out of the rind that would otherwise get tossed in the garbage. It's the ultimate waste-not, want-not recipe. I use them on top of tacos, and he loved chopping them into bits and using them as a relish on burgers and hot dogs.

MAKES 2½ PINTS (578 GRAMS)

1½ cups (337 ml) apple cider vinegar

¾ cup (150 grams) granulated natural cane sugar

4 cups (472 grams) washed watermelon rind, thinly sliced (about 3-inch/7-cm-long pieces)

1 medium jalapeño, thinly sliced

½ teaspoon whole all spice berries

Freshly grated zest of 1 lime

Add the vinegar and sugar to a deep glass microwave-safe bowl. Cook on high power until it comes to a boil, about 6 minutes. Add the remaining ingredients, stir well, and cook on high for 2 more minutes. Spoon the pickled rind into tightly sealed glass jars and store in the fridge for up to 2 months (they're ready to eat as soon as they're thoroughly chilled), or process in a hot water bath for 10 minutes for long-term storage in your dry goods pantry (page 215).

> **SAFETY FIRST!** While the acid in the vinegar is powerful enough to safely preserve your pickles, I prefer not to take any chances by introducing germs. Don't use the eaten-up rinds that are covered in drool. Instead, cut up your watermelon, trimming off the rinds first, and save those to make these pickles. The rinds will keep fresh for 2 days in a plastic zip-top bag, so they don't have to be made the same day you cut up the watermelon.

GRILLED GARLIC SCAPE PESTO

Most people are accustomed to using garlic bulbs in cooking, but the tops of the plants, called garlic scapes, are just as edible. On first bite, they seem to be a little more mellow than raw garlic cloves, but a few seconds later the vibrant peppery punch sneaks up on you. My answer to taming the flavor is grilling them and making this pesto with toasted pistachios, which have a sweeter flavor than most other nuts. Virginia used to eat this by the spoonful when she was just a year old. It's also delicious smeared on toasted baguette, added in dollops to poached eggs (page 58), tossed with hot pasta, or paired with grilled skirt steak—a Mikey favorite.

MAKES 1 CUP (230 GRAMS)

10 garlic scapes
½ cup (56 grams) freshly grated Parmesan cheese
⅓ cup (44 grams) shelled, unsalted pistachios, toasted
½ cup (125 ml) extra-virgin olive oil, plus more as needed
Freshly ground black pepper

Preheat a gas grill. Cook the scapes, turning frequently, until they are slightly charred all over, about 3 minutes. Alternatively, you can broil them: preheat your broiler. Place the scapes on a baking sheet, and cook them, turning frequently, until slightly charred all over, 2 to 3 minutes.

Add the scapes, cheese, and pistachios to the bowl of a food processor. Pulse until the scapes and nuts are very finely chopped. Slowly add the olive oil, while pulsing, until it forms a wet paste. Season with black pepper to taste.

Add more oil if you desire a wetter pesto, especially if tossing with pasta.

EGG-FREE · V · MAKE AHEAD · GLUTEN-FREE · 30 MINUTES OR LESS

SALTED MOLASSES BUTTER

A hot, flaky biscuit slathered with butter seems indulgent for breakfast, but I must admit it's one of my favorites. One morning I went out to Seersucker, a restaurant in Carroll Gardens, Brooklyn, for breakfast with a group of friends after we dropped our kids off at school. When the plate of hot biscuits came to the table, we all inspected the salted molasses butter that arrived alongside them in a tiny pot. One taste, and the oohs and ahhs flowed freely. Someone said, "I wonder how you'd make it at home?" I promptly replied, "It's easy—just mix together some softened butter with molasses!"

MAKES ½ CUP (119 GRAMS)

1 stick (112 grams) unsalted butter, at room temperature
1 teaspoon (7 grams) unsulphured molasses (I use Wholesome Sweeteners)
Generous pinch of sea salt

Add all the ingredients to a deep bowl. Vigorously whisk them together until well combined. Transfer the butter to a ramekin or small glass jar, cover, and store in the refrigerator for up to 1 week.

WHOLE GRAIN MUSTARD

The day I decided to make homemade mustard, I wasn't sure if I should also check myself in for a mental evaluation. It's not at all hard to do, but it's more the circumstances under which I decided to undertake the project. I had a smidge of store-bought mustard left in the fridge. Rather than just buying a new jar, I decided to make my own using the extra mustard seeds I had in the pantry from all my pickling projects. The crazy part is that it meant I wouldn't have mustard for two weeks, since it needs time to mellow out—freshly made mustard is quite abrasive, and doesn't have the nuanced flavors of an aged one. When Mikey came home that night, I announced that there would be no mustard for two weeks, and told him why. His reply was, "When are you going to start making your own water?"

MAKES 1 CUP (250 GRAMS)

Scant $\frac{1}{3}$ cup (82 grams) mix of yellow and brown mustard seeds

$\frac{1}{4}$ cup (22 grams) mustard powder (I use Coleman's)

Scant $\frac{1}{2}$ cup (115 ml) cold filtered water

2 tablespoons (30 ml) white vinegar

1 tablespoon (15 ml) sherry vinegar

2 tablespoons (42 grams) honey

$\frac{3}{4}$ teaspoon (4 grams) fine sea salt

Add the mustard seeds to a food processor and pulse until about two-thirds of the seeds are coarsely ground.

In a small bowl, stir together the mustard powder and water with a fork. Pour in the vinegars, honey, and salt, mixing well to combine. Stir in the mustard seeds. The mixture will look more like a slurry at first, but it will thicken after a few days.

Transfer the mustard to a jar, seal it tightly, and store in the fridge. Let it "cure" for 2 weeks, to allow the flavors to soften and develop, before using.

HOMEMADE MAYONNAISE

Most cooks love their immersion blenders for puréeing soups, but for me it's invaluable for making mayonnaise from scratch. I've tried it in the blender and food processor, both of which did the job well, but it's a fussy process that requires adding oil one drop at a time. Then my friend John, who founded the blog FoodWishes.com, posted a video for making mayo with an immersion blender in just two minutes—no joke! I decided to keep my original ingredients and simply use his technique. Don't tell him I said this, but he's a genius.

MAKES ABOUT ¾ CUP (190 GRAMS)

1 large egg yolk (save the white for a later use)

1 tablespoon (15 ml) freshly squeezed lemon juice

¼ teaspoon (1 gram) fine sea salt, plus more to taste

½ teaspoon (2 grams) smooth Dijon mustard (not whole grain)

¾ cup (187 ml) canola oil

In this exact order, add the egg yolk, lemon juice, salt, mustard, and oil to a tall measuring cup. Let the ingredients sit for 1 minute, as the egg yolk settles to the bottom.

Place the immersion blender into the cup and slowly start pulsing the mixture. In a few seconds you will see the mayo begin to form at the bottom and little bubbles of mayo float to the top. You can move the immersion blender gently up and down to finish making the mayo. The whole process should take about 1 minute. Scrape the mayonnaise into a container, cover it tightly, and store in the fridge for up to 3 days.

Variation: Naturally Low-fat Mayonnaise

You can get great-tasting mayo without the egg yolk, and save some calories, too. Substitute 1 large egg white for the egg yolk, ¼ teaspoon dry mustard (I use Colman's) for the Dijon, and reduce the oil to ½ cup (125 ml). Layer all the ingredients as directed for Homemade Mayonnaise, and proceed with the remainder of the recipe. You can store low-fat mayonnaise in the fridge for up to 3 days.

> **STORING EGG WHITES AND YOLKS** Egg whites will last for up to 1 week in the fridge in a tightly sealed container, or up to 1 month in the freezer (thaw them overnight in the fridge before using). Egg yolks are a bit more perishable. Store them in a tightly sealed container in the fridge, with a piece of plastic wrap placed directly on top of the yolk so it doesn't dry out and form a skin. They will last for up to 2 days this way.

MAKE AHEAD GLUTEN-FREE V PANTRY BASICS 30 MINUTES OR LESS DAIRY-FREE

HOT FUDGE SAUCE

Sundaes just aren't complete without hot fudge, so I set out to create a recipe for one that everyone could enjoy: hence no heavy cream or butter. You'll never miss the dairy in this rich, thick chocolate sauce perfect for pouring on top of any frozen treat—or just eating by the spoonful if your will power is as weak as mine.

MAKES 1¼ CUPS (200 GRAMS)

½ cup (100 grams) granulated natural cane sugar

9 ounces (255 grams) bittersweet chocolate (72%), finely chopped

Pinch of fine sea salt

2 tablespoons (30 ml) brown rice syrup

1 teaspoon (5 ml) vanilla extract

Combine the sugar in a small saucepan with ½ cup of water. Bring to a boil over medium-high heat. Cook for 2 minutes until the sugar is completely dissolved and the liquid is syrupy.

Meanwhile, place the chocolate in a deep heatproof bowl and add the salt. Pour the sugar syrup over the chocolate, and let it sit undisturbed for 1 to 2 minutes to melt the chocolate. Stir with a rubber spatula until the chocolate is melted—don't worry that it looks a little thick, and almost curdled. Stir in the brown rice syrup and vanilla extract. The sauce will become glossy and smooth, but still stay thick.

Pour into a glass jar and let cool completely. Cover tightly and store in the fridge for up to 1 month. It will harden in the fridge—don't worry. To use, scoop some of the solid hot fudge sauce into a bowl and heat it in the microwave, using 15-second intervals, until it is smooth and pourable.

WHAT IS BROWN RICE SYRUP? This sweetener is a healthier alternative to corn syrup, and is my go-to swap-in for any recipe that calls for it.

BASIC VINAIGRETTE

I was on the fence about including such a basic dressing, but noticed that most of my friends and family buy vinaigrette dressings at the supermarket. The secret to my dressing is honey. A little bit goes a long way in balancing out the bracing acidity of the vinegar. Chefs will tell you to slowly whisk the olive oil in to create an emulsion, but the truth is that giving all the ingredients a good shake in a jar does the trick just fine and makes for easy storage and cleanup.

MAKES ¾ CUP (187 ML)

¹/₄ cup (2 ounces) red wine vinegar

1 tablespoon (21 grams) honey

1 teaspoon (2 grams) Whole Grain Mustard (page 227)

¹/₂ cup (125 ml) extra-virgin olive oil

Fine sea salt and freshly ground black pepper

Add the vinegar, honey, mustard, and olive oil to a glass jar with a lid. Tightly seal the jar and shake vigorously until it is well combined and smooth. Season the dressing with salt and pepper to taste. Store the vinaigrette in the sealed jar for up to 1 month. Give it a good shake each time before using it.

MAKE IT YOUR OWN! All salad dressings need an acid to create a balance—in this case it's red wine vinegar. You can put your own twist on it by using half red wine vinegar and half apple cider vinegar, freshly squeezed lemon juice, or orange juice for a citrus vinaigrette. For a more intensely flavored dressing, try swapping in balsamic vinegar for all the red wine vinegar.

EGG-FREE · PANTRY BASICS · MAKE AHEAD · GLUTEN-FREE · V · DAIRY-FREE · 30 MINUTES OR LESS

OREGANO & ORANGE ZEST OLIVE OIL

Infused olive oils are easy to make, and are a great way to preserve fresh herbs and spruce up your bread basket. My girls love dipping chunks of bread in this one. I also like to drizzle it over sliced tomatoes or chunks of fresh mozzarella, or even toss it with pasta and a sprinkling of hot chili pepper flakes for a quick weeknight dinner. If you can't find fresh oregano, try using lemon thyme or swapping in 2 sprigs of fresh rosemary instead.

MAKES ½ CUP (125 ML)

¹/₂ cup (125 ml) extra-virgin olive oil

2-inch (5-cm) piece of orange rind, very thinly sliced

¹/₄ cup (5 grams) fresh oregano, roughly chopped

Pinch of fine sea salt

Freshly ground black pepper

Add the olive oil to a small pot or skillet over medium heat. Heat the oil until it becomes fragrant. Add the orange rind and oregano, and cook for 30 seconds. Remove the pot from the heat, and season with salt and pepper to taste. Pour the oil into a jar and let it cool. Cover and store in the fridge; use within 1 week.

HOMEMADE *with* Love

BOOZY WET WALNUTS

When I was a kid, my mom and I used to love going to Carvel on
Wednesdays for the "buy one, get one free" sundae special. I always picked vanilla ice cream
with hot fudge and wet walnuts. I'd almost forgotten about those days until I made the hot fudge
recipe for this book (page 230). The memories came flooding back, and prompted this updated
version of those wet walnuts with a splash of bourbon to mark my entry into adulthood.

MAKES 2 CUPS (350 GRAMS)

½ cup (100 grams) granulated natural cane sugar

½ teaspoon vanilla extract

⅓ cup (100 grams) brown rice syrup

1½ cups (131 grams) shelled unsalted walnuts, chopped

Splash of bourbon

Add the sugar and ½ cup (125 ml) of water to a 2-quart (2.2-L) pot. Bring to a boil over medium
heat. Cook until the sugar is completely dissolved, about 2 minutes. Whisk in the vanilla extract
and brown rice syrup. Stir in the walnuts and bourbon, and reduce the heat to medium-low. Simmer for 5 minutes to infuse the walnuts with the bourbon flavor.

Spoon the walnuts into a clean glass jar and let them cool completely. Cover with a lid and store
in the fridge for up to 1 month.

MAKE IT KID-FRIENDLY If you want the kids to enjoy this sundae topping, then just
omit the bourbon and follow the recipe as directed. This alcohol-free version also makes
a great add-in for yogurt.

HOMEMADE CHOCOLATE SYRUP

I enjoy an icy cold glass of chocolate milk as much as my daughters do, perhaps even more so, which is what first inspired me to make chocolate syrup. On the night I set out to create this recipe, my friend Sarah's son Oliver popped into my mind. He's allergic to cow's milk, and it made me think long and hard about how to make a dairy-free chocolate syrup he could enjoy, too. Stir this into the milk of your choosing—soy, almond, and coconut all work deliciously—or drizzle it over your favorite ice cream for a happy ending to a long day.

MAKES ¾ CUP (187 ML)

¹⁄₂ cup (100 grams) granulated natural cane sugar
2 tablespoons (14 grams) dark cocoa powder (I use Valrhona)
¹⁄₂ teaspoon vanilla extract

Add the sugar along with ¹⁄₂ cup (125 ml) of water to a 2-quart (2.2-L) pot. Bring to a boil, and cook for 2 minutes until the sugar has completely dissolved and is thick and syrupy.

Reduce the heat to low. Whisk in the cocoa powder and vanilla extract until the cocoa is completely dissolved. Cook for 1 minute more. The syrup will be thin and liquidy.

Transfer to a glass jar and set on the counter to cool completely. Store, tightly sealed, in the fridge for up to 3 months. Shake well before each use.

GLUTEN-FREE · VEGAN · MAKE AHEAD · 30 MINUTES OR LESS · PANTRY BASICS

Index

Note: Page references in *italics* indicate recipe photographs.

239

INDEX

HOMEMADE
with
Love

More Advance Praise for *Homemade with Love,* by Jennifer Perillo:

"The proper way to read Jennifer Perillo's *Homemade with Love*
is curled up in a crocheted blanket your grandmother made, on a comfy couch
with a cup of tea or hot chocolate. It's that kind of book. With gentle prose,
simple and delightful recipes that should be in every home cook's repertoire,
and beautifully photographed, this book is one you will cherish."

—ELISE BAUER, CREATOR OF SIMPLYRECIPES.COM

"This new how-to bible on cooking from scratch surprises you because
it's so much more. Jennie reinvents the classics of our Brooklyn youths, ensuring
these homemade recipes are enjoyed by a more health-conscious generation.
To top it off you can create delicious meals without laboring in the kitchen for hours!"

—ISABEL KALLMAN, FOUNDER OF ALPHA MOM

"If you are a fan of Jennie's wonderful blog, you probably have already
grabbed up copies of this lovely book for yourself and everyone you love.
If you are new to Jennie, you will soon see why she is so popular. Reassuring,
unassuming, deeply knowledgeable, open, and as passionate about people as she is
about cooking, Jennie will leave her mark on your kitchen and in your heart."

—MOLLIE KATZEN, AUTHOR OF *THE MOOSEWOOD COOKBOOK*

"Jennie Perillo's accessible collection of comforting, everyday recipes will inspire even
the most reluctant cook. I, for one, can't wait to add things like her Lentil-Ricotta "Meatballs,"
Olive Oil and Feta Mashed Turnips, and Apricot Butter to my permanent repertoire."

—LUISA WEISS, AUTHOR OF *MY BERLIN KITCHEN*
AND CREATOR OF THE WEDNESDAY CHEF